DISCLAIMER

The material in this book is for information purpose only and not intended as a substitute for the advice and care of your Doctor. If you have been diagnosed with Iron Deficiency Anaemia(IDA) and on prescribed medication, please do not stop taking them.

Anyone with food allergy or intolerance is strongly advised to consult with their Doctor or Medical Practitioner before trying out any of the recipes in this book.

The cooking times given for each recipe are an approximate guide only. The methods used may differ according to the techniques and equipment used by different people.

DEDICATION

In loving memory of my father Justice J.P.C Nganje who instilled in me the importance of education and hard work. He taught me to believe in myself, stand for what is right, be true to myself, help others wherever possible and be respectful to others.

Daddy when we used to talk and spend time together which was very often you always told me never to give up on my writing. You supported me and always encouraged me to carry on writing and to make sure it gets published. I have finally done it but sadly you did not live to celebrate this wonderful achievement with me. I Thank you for being the best father and a very dedicated one too. RIP Dad you light shines forever in my heart and your legacy lives on.

Table of Contents

Why I Have Written This Book..1

Introduction..3

The Symptoms Of Iron Deficiency Anaemia I Experienced........11

PART 1 BOOSTING BREAKFAST 16

    Seasonal Fresh Fruits with Natural Yoghurt..............................18

    Lovely Apple Banana and Prune Smoothie 20

    Simply Fruit & Veg Smoothie 21

    Toasted Crumpets with Stewed berries......................................22

    Wholemeal Bread with Crunchy Peanut Butter & Banana........24

    African-Style Spicy Hot Scrambled Egg with Kale..................25

    Gracious Pancakes with Dark Cocoa Powder...........................26

    Tasty French Baguette with Avocado 28

    Curried Bake Beans on Toast..30

    Fruity Breakfast Muffins...34

PART 2 UPLIFTING LIGHT LUNCHES 36

    Vibrant Jacket Potato with Cheese..37

    Mind-Blowing Coleslaw 39

    Jazzed-Up Instant Noodles..41

    Scrumptious Quinoa with Tuna Salad 43

    Enchanting salad with Prawns 45

    Delicious Lentils and Butternut Squash Soup...........................47

    Glorious Green Salad with Avocado & Pumpkin Seeds...........49

    Broccoli Curly Kale and Carrot Soup 51

Pitta Bread Pockets with Chicken Salad 52

Sizzling Oven Cooked Vegetables with smoked Mackerel Fillets 54

French Stick Pizza..56

Mixed Root Vegetable Salad 57

PART 3 HEARTY MAIN MEALS 59

Jollof Rice with Sardines and Chickpeas....................60

Wheatgerm Coated Sticky Chicken Wings..................62

Chickpeas Curry..64

Mix Bean Curry 65

Easy Fried Rice with Shrimps....................................67

Truly Irritable Dry-Fried Ox Liver 69

Aromatic Chicken Curry with Coconut Milk 71

Succulent Parcel-Baked Salmon Fillet........................73

Wow - Factor Spaghetti 'N' Mince............................75

Flavourful sautéed Spinach with Boiled Green Plantains..........77

Mouth-Watering Beef Casserole...............................79

Roasted Sweet Potato Boats with Mixed Vegetables 80

Grilled Chicken Fillets Mash and Lentils 82

Mixed Fried Cabbage with Tofu................................84

Exciting Spinach and mushroom Rice 85

Curried Quinoa with Kale 87

Unapologetic Vegetable Lasagne...............................89

One-Pot Potato with chicken.....................................91

Speedy and Fragrant Couscous 93

Meat-Free Sweet Potato Pie.....................................94

Tasty Tuna Pasta Bake 96

PART 4 SWEET SENSATIONS...97

Tropical Fruits with Natural Wheat-Germ Yoghurt 98

Fruit Cocktail Jelly 99

Spiced Baked Apples 100

Dark Chocolate Chip and Banana Muffins 101

No-Bake Strawberry Cheese Cake..103

Indulging Apple Crumble 105

Coconut and Dark Chocolate Chip Frozen Yoghurt................107

Colourful Fruit Salad 108

Stewed Berries with Cream...109

Roasted Seasonal Fruits 110

PART 5 THIRST QUENCHERS 111

Refreshing Spinach Drink...112

Carrot and Beetroot Smoothie..113

Heavenly Smoothie 114

Morning Glory 115

Tropical Passion..116

Start- My-Day Smoothie 117

Fruits in Season Smoothie...118

Warm Dark Cocoa Drink 119

Fresh Pineapple and Watermelon Drink 120

Adam and Eve Drink...121

PART 6 HOW I ATE ON A TYPICAL DAY**..................................122**

Breakfast 122

My Tips On How I Managed Iron Deficiency Aneamia For a Better Well-Being..124

Some Key Points To Remember..131

Conclusion 133

Useful Information...136

Aknowledgements 137

About The Author...138

WHY I HAVE WRITTEN THIS BOOK

Dear Reader,

I am happy that you are reading my book and thank you for making that choice. I believe that you may have been diagnosed with iron deficiency anaemia or know someone who has the reason why you are seeking to gain more information. I can tell you now that you have chosen the right book. I am a Health Promotion Officer and work in the primary prevention sector. My main job role is to educate and raise awareness to the target communities identified as being at risk of certain health related illnesses. I encourage people to make informed choices and change lifestyle habits in beneficial ways for a better wellbeing. I am not a Medical Doctor and so cannot give advice or prescribe treatment on any condition. What I can do is to equip you with more knowledge about Iron Deficiency Anaemia (IDA) and how you can do things differently to elevate the symptoms and boost your iron levels like I did.

I have written this book with the aim of sharing my experience of IDA and how I supplemented my prescribed medication with iron-boosting natural foods to improve my health and well-being. My intension is to educate, inspire and motivate anyone in a similar situation to take responsibility of their health, make informed choices and positive changes to their lifestyle. The recipes in this book will provide you with new ideas on how to combine different foods to help boost up your iron levels. After my diagnosis I struggled to find iron rich recipes that really catered for my African palate (Taste, flavour, spice and texture). I read about my condition extensively and was able to find most of the answers to the questions that baffled me about Iron Deficiency Anaemia. As I read through several stories and reviews it became clear to me that there were also other people from different backgrounds seeking a solution to the same problem I had. In my desperation to improve my well-being with natural foods I began to plan my meals on the foods that were high in iron whilst maintaining a nutritious and balanced diet. Creating, testing and writing up recipes became a regular and therapeutic activity for me. My family and close friends became very good at giving me honest feedback and I always offered to cook a dish whenever I got invited to a party. This meant that I received different opinions which were what I needed to perfect the recipes. This book has recipes with influence and flavours from other parts of the world because I love and enjoy cooking a wide variety of foods adding my own twist to it. The recipes in this book are some of my favourites that I prepared most of the time. Its wide ranging, varied and versatile so you can use your imagination and turn them into your own creations. The ingredients used can be bought from any supermarket or ethnic food store. Eating a variety of natural iron boosting foods was one of the best decisions I ever made. I hope that as you read through this book you will be able to find some useful information and ideas that will improve your iron intake and help you on your way to good health.

Good Luck,

Cathy

INTRODUCTION

My story

Hands up! If you have ever ignored any feeling of tiredness, headache or dizziness blaming it on everyday work stresses? Yes! My hands are up too because I am as guilty as anyone else. I had been feeling unwell for a very long time with reoccurring cold and cough, regular dizziness, tiredness and light headedness which interfered greatly with my everyday activities. I struggled with these discomforts but carried on as normal hoping that it will get better with the help of some home remedies I was using at the time. It did not help much because my symptoms became persistent and unbearable and as time progressed I became very unwell.

On one cold November day in 2014 I felt very sick and had to go to the clinic for consultation. Dressed up in a black long winter jacket and a thick woollen scarf wrapped round my neck I walked slowly with both my hands tucked fully into my pockets for warmth. I coughed constantly and the ten minutes distance from my house to the clinic left me feeling out of breath and exhausted. I arrived at the clinic with just a few minutes to spare before my appointment time and was able to sit down to regain my breath and strength. My main intention that day was to get some antibiotics for my persistent cold and cough. I was certain that was what I needed to get rid of my cold. I had become my own doctor. I felt relieved and secured knowing that I was in the right place and my prescription of antibiotics was now within reach. In the consultation room I sat patiently on the edge of the chair and watched as the Doctor punched the keyboard heavily with one finger in search of my details. After a couple of minutes, he spun his big black chair around fully acknowledging my presence with some opening questions. "Why have you come to see me today"? he asked. Look straight at him and replied, "I have come for some antibiotics because I have been suffering from persistent cold and cough for over six months despite having been taking some remedies from the pharmacy". "How is your health in general"? was the next question that followed. "I have good and bad days but feel generally well otherwise". I did not know if what I said made any sense because he remained silent and looked back on his computer screen. I carried on telling him in detail all I could say about my bad days. Dizziness, light headedness, episodes of blackouts, weakness, shortness of breath and all I could remember.

His face had no expression except for a steady stare. He took a deep breath and said in a quiet tone "I will have to send you for a blood test". He got hold of the mouse and with a few clicks handed over a slip of paper from the printer on which he had ticked a few boxes. I felt disappointed that I did not get any antibiotics just some leaflets with plenty of tips and advice on keeping well in the cold weather. I glanced at the slip as I walked out of the consultation room but was unable to make sense of what he had ticked. I headed straight to the blood department which was packed full of people that were also waiting to be seen for various reasons I presumed. The room was quiet and the atmosphere miserable except for the constant ringing of the phones and the receptionist getting on with her job. It looked stressful as she struggled to joggle many things at a time. There were no smiles, no happy faces, no conversations just the odd grim, fidgeting and coughing. I waited patiently with my allocated number in my hand and glanced occasionally around the room just to be aware of my surroundings. I kept my mind busy by reading some of the magazines I had picked up from the table. The stories were interesting, some funny and some sad but the agony aunt pages took my mind off my own problem for a short while. As I buried myself in the pages of other people's problems I was unexpectedly distracted by the loud crying of an infant boy which appeared to be the right solution to dilute the tense atmosphere because it got heads turning around and eyes rolling in a questionable manner. The baby's cry was loud and got louder as he twitched his body and kicked the air with his tiny and cute legs. He must be in some sort of pain I thought to myself and watched from about four chairs away as his mother tried hard to make him comfortable. She appeared to be uncomfortable with the situation and I could also sense the negative body language of the other patients in the room, the typical eye and head movements accompanied with shrugging of the shoulder – a common British form of communicating their frustration. I heard the ding-dong sound and saw my name flashing on the electronic caller display which meant it was my time to see the nurse. I followed the signs through a maze-like corridor into a room. The nurse was very chatty and appeared happy. It was clear to me that she had found ways of making her job interesting and exciting or perhaps it was just her personality. Whatever the case I immediately felt at ease. I sat in a big black leather chair with my left arm stretched out and sleeve rolled up neatly. She tied a rubber band round my left arm and tapped lightly with her index finger in search of a vein. "Make a tight fist". she said to me. I did as I was told but there was no luck with that arm. "What have you done with your veins?" She joked and looked up at me. "I asked them to go into hiding" was my reply and we both laughed. Right let's try the other arm, shall we? Same process all over again and a vein was staring right back at her. "Ah! Good" she said with some relief. "All you will feel is a sharp scratch from the needle." she said and at that point I looked away and I am sure most people with the fear of needles will do the same. "This is an easy flow you seem to have a lot of blood. Have you ever considered blood donation?" She asked me. "No but will think about it". In approximately two minutes she had filled up three small blood bottles on which she labelled and placed on a small tray and gave me a small cotton wool to place over the area to stop the bleeding.

All done now, and the results will be sent to your doctor within 3-5 days. Thank you and I walked out of the room in good spirits. When I got outside of the clinic I decided to take a walk around the shopping centre before heading home because I was in a happy mood and wanted to kill off sometime. The question the nurse had asked me earlier about blood donation played on my mind and I decided I will have it on my to-do list for when I get well. I got back home in the evening and settled down to a bowl of spicy hot African chicken Stew with boiled white rice and mixed vegetables. The television was on in the background as I savoured every mouthful of rice. It had just gone past 7.00 pm when my phone rang with a private caller ID. I hesitated for a moment but quickly swallowed what I had in my mouth and took the call. It was a male voice. Hello, is that Catherine? Yessss! I dragged the word not sure of what to expect because I did not recognise the voice as he said, I am one of the doctors from the clinic where you had your bloods taken earlier. By this time my heart had begun to beat faster. I remained silent as he spoke with some urgency in his voice. Your blood results are not very good, and I have made an urgent referral for you at the hospital. You will have to go at once to the accident and emergency department at the Queen Elizabeth hospital and make sure you do not drive. Doctor what do you mean I asked him? "Your Haemoglobin level is 6.0, dangerously low and would require urgent medical attention. I have forwarded all the required information to the A & E department". It was a brief call and as I hung up the phone I was worried and unclear about the condition and its complications. By this time my dinner had gone very cold and I had completely lost my appetite as panic took over me.

In this state, I called my children who were home with me at the time and gave them the news. They were visibly worried and as expected began to bombard me with a lot of questions to enhance their own understanding of what was happening. I could see fear in their eyes, the sought of fear we all have experienced at some point in our younger lives when we saw that a parent was not well. I kept the answers very simple and reassuring. My children were very supportive and helpful in whatever way they were able to. Preparing for the unknown I decided to pack an overnight bag and got a lift to the hospital. The accident and emergency department were full of people and very busy as always. On arrival I walked straight to the reception desk and gave my name. My details were brought up on the computer screen and I was asked to confirm my details as a normal procedure. For the first time I did not have to wait around for long before I was called in. Ten minutes instead of the usual three hours wait was a pleasant feeling. I felt like a special guest. I was truly happy with the express service which is not usually the case with the A& E department and most people will identify with this. I followed the nurse as she walked hurriedly through the winding corridors behind the scenes. I struggled to keep up with her pace just like a child trotting faster to catch up with an adult in a hurry. The busy back scenes of the A&E can only be compared to the famous never sleeping Oxford Street in central London. Doctors and nurses criss-crossed one another often in a hurry tightly clutching onto large files and papers. The clanging of the medical machines, the non-stop ringing of the phones and bleeps gave the true meaning of the words emergency department -a place where every second counts. The constant sounds from the phones, bleeps and machines appeared to be the music in the ward with no rhythm but somehow sounded good. It was a welcomed distraction. I was taken into one of the cubicles which had a bed, a chair and side table where I was seen by a doctor for a brief introduction and he left to return later leaving the nurse to carry on with the routine observations.

The curtains of the cubicle were drawn but through a peep-hole opening I was able to see the doctors standing by the nurse's station talking and flipping over the pages of a voluminous brown tired-looking file. I could not hear what they were saying but assumed they were discussing my case as one of them pointed to the cubicle in which I was sitting. I took my eyes off the peep-hole for some minutes and without notice a tall slim build and soft-spoken doctor came in holding the same big brown file I had spotted earlier. He smiled and introduced himself and, in a joking, tone said, so you are the trouble maker. I smiled back and from that moment the grip of anxiousness left me, and I was ready for what he had to tell me. He glanced briefly at my medical notes and said, "what have you been doing with your blood?" I chuckled and replied, "I don't know where it's gone to and that's why I am here for you to find it". Don't worry he said, you are in the right place. I knew that already but needed reassurance from a clinician. Now tell me about what you would do on a typical day. Doctor I have a long list of things I would normally do daily but will summarise it as this, I go to work, cook dinner, housekeeping, do some work on the computer and on some days go to the gym after work. Gym? He repeated and looked at me in shock. "How have you been doing it?" He asked. If I had a Haemoglobin level (HB)of 6.0I would be sleeping all day. He went on to explain in the simplest of terms the meaning of iron deficiency anaemia (IDA) with just four words– low-red-blood-cells. This means that your iron levels are lower than normal. I listened attentively as he explained with simple words. Iron is needed by the body for healthy blood cells which carries oxygen around the body. You do not have sufficient iron in your body that's why you have been feeling tired and dizzy combined with all the other symptoms. What a simple explanation I thought to myself. I was very happy to have finally had a clear understanding of my condition without any complicated medical jargon. After a short pause to allow me to take it all in he continued to say that the recommended course of treatment in my case would be blood transfusion which will be the quickest way to get me out of the danger zone. You can also be treated with tablets but with your HB levels dangerously low it will not be effective in terms of quick results which is what is required in your case. Think about it and I will come back in a few minutes. When he left the word dangerously low kept ringing in my ears like the chimes of Big Ben on New Year's Eve in London. The words dangerously low scared me because that was the second time I had been told that from two different doctors on the same day. It was worrying. Thinking about my options I was leaning more towards having a blood transfusion because I had been through it before. By the time he came back I was ready with my response. I will go with blood transfusion I told him. That's fine he replied and that means we will have to keep you in hospital overnight and treatment will start immediately. I was not worried about staying the night because I came prepared and getting back to my normal healthy self was my number one priority. He left to feedback to his team and later that evening I was allocated a bed in the ward where my treatment of four units of blood transfusion commenced. The nurses were busy but friendly and tried hard to respond to the constant ringing of the patient's bedsides alarm and the phones ringing. With nothing much to do, I laid on my bed feeling bored and began counting the blood as it dropped and trickled slowly down the tiny tube into my vein. That kept my mind occupied for a while until I fell asleep. Treatment was completed in the evening of the following day and the next morning I was seen by the doctor who informed me that my blood levels had not reached the expected levels but was satisfactory and safer than what it was before. I was a little bit disappointed but on the other hand was happy to get out of the danger zone. The doctor prescribed some iron tablets and advised me to eat lots of iron rich foods to get my levels up. He also requested for the dietician to see me before discharge. I was happy to be set free after two nights with plenty of iron tablets, advice, tips and information on iron rich foods.

From that moment I knew I had a big part to play in my recovery in terms of diet and lifestyle change. Taking ferrous sulphate tablets three times a day was not something I enjoyed doing. I knew I did not want to be on long term medication, so it was the start of my special relationship with iron rich foods and health shops. Before my diagnosis I maintained an active and busy life running my own errands, joggling between work, family and social life and even finding the time to throw in some gym workout three to four days a week. At the end of the day I used to feel completely drained, short of breath and very weak but always used to put it down to overworking and over stretching myself. Little did I know that I was suffering from Iron Deficiency Anaemia. When I look back now I am glad that I went to see the doctor although it took a few years. Part of me regrets not listening to my body well enough and ignoring all the classic symptoms that should have pushed me to go to the clinic earlier. I made my health less of a priority and put every other need before mine. They say it's in a woman's nature to do so and I also believe that we were made that way but Hey! Ladies don't you all think that it's time we start looking after ourselves too and paying more attention to the unusual signs and signals from our bodies?

THE SYMPTOMS OF IRON DEFICIECIENCY ANAEMIA I EXPERIENCED

I had been experiencing these combinations of symptoms long before I was diagnosed with Iron Deficiency Anaemia and for over a year I relied heavily on home remedies which helped temporarily in relieving some of the symptoms. I will share with you the symptoms I experienced daily until my condition was finally picked up by a routine blood test.

REOCCURING COUGH AND COLD

I suffered from cold and cough throughout the year and felt feverish even when the temperatures were very warm. This made me dressed in warm clothing and always kept my jumper on. Warm clothing in summer is something you do not come across very often. I felt out of place as it appeared like fashion had left me behind. I made regular visits to my local pharmacy for cough and cold remedies and even made some friends as a regular customer. Being on first name terms with the pharmacist made me feel very special because there was always time for a chat. Bonus!

Apart from my trips to the pharmacy I also did my own home treatment of boiled fresh ginger and lemon tea and my granny's trusted treatment of inhaling the Vicks menthol rub in hot water with a sheet or blanket over my head. It helped because it gave me some temporary relieve.

CONSTANTLY FEELING TIRED AND EXCHAUSTED

Tiredness and weakness can become part of a busy daily routine especially when you have early starts and late nights, something I have been doing for many years. Such a non-stop routine is bound to affect the health and well-being of anyone. Occasionally I would break off for some rest to regain my strength when feeling burnout. It became problematic when tiredness and weakness kept reoccurring even at those times when I was not doing much more than I would normally do. This was interfering with my daily performance especially after an activity and even after a long rest I would still not be in the mood to carry on and yawned constantly. I am usually a very energetic and an on-and-about person not known for taking naps during the day, but my condition was wearing me thin physically and mentally. I found myself losing touch with my surroundings and struggled with the simplest of tasks such as shopping, housekeeping and walking long distances or up a flight of stairs. As a mother I bravely carried on with my motherly responsibilities and maintained a positive attitude - something women are very skilled at doing. Once again, I am tempted to say that it is in our nature as women to always stay strong in challenging times and I am sure you would agree with me on this.

PALE AND WASHED-OUT APPEARANCE

I am of a light skin tone, natural glow with a bubbly personality always laughing and making jokes. All of that disappeared, leaving me looking completely washed-out. My close family and friends became very concerned. It was tough for me because I did not have answers to the questions that kept rolling in about my appearance. In my defence I became very good at dismissing their concerns and blaming it on not having enough rest. They were not convinced by the looks on their faces but somehow let it go. On one occasion a close family member who had had enough of my excuses gave me a right telling off. In a stern tone she said, "I think it is time you see your doctor before it's too late because you look sick". That hit a nerve because it got me thinking. She was right after all.

REGULAR SHORTNESS OF BREATH

I experienced shortness of breath daily and it was sometimes scary and made me feel anxious often thinking I was going to die. It often occurred when I engaged in any sort of activity that needed me to use up more energy than usual such as housekeeping, walking up the stairs or hilly road, running for the bus or train. This was limiting for me in so many ways and each day was different. I felt trapped.

LOW CONCENTRATION LEVELS

My levels of concentration dropped drastically, and I found myself being easily distracted. I became angry. Irritated and frustrated with everything around me for no good reason. I also lost interest and motivation in some of the things I regularly did such as browsing the shops for clothes, shoes and handbags, cooking and baking. Night times were very difficult because I found it hard to go to sleep and when I did I will wake up in the early hours of the morning unable to go back to sleep. This unplanned routine left me feeling very tired in the mornings and throughout the day. I became grumpy, emotional and reacted slower than usual. It was a constant struggle for me especially with my mood. I had lost touch with myself – a very frustrating experience at the time.

EPISODES OF DIZZINESS AND BLACKOUTS

Dizziness and short spells of blackouts were a regular occurrence for me especially when standing up suddenly from a sitting or resting position. This usually lasted a few minutes leaving me feeling disorientated and uncomfortable and sometimes with some short sharp pain in my head. During the summer season when the temperatures became warm my symptoms became worst. I could not enjoy the sunshine because I was always seeking for shelter when out. I felt miserable and out of place and must admit that I was very jealous of those who were making the most of the warm weather.

CRAVING FOR ICE CUBES

I constantly craved and chewed on ice cubes no matter the time of the year. I carried ice cubes with me in a sandwich bag most times when out and about. Yes, it sounds weird I know but it was a way of getting rid of the funny taste, dryness and soreness I felt in my mouth. When out eating in restaurants I always requested for an extra glass of ice. My family and friends found my chronic ice-chewing habit very bizarre especially in the winter season. My dentist also noticed that the constant crushing of ice cubes was affecting my teeth. I planned to stop on several occasions but found it extremely difficult. I had no idea that low iron levels were the cause of my strange craving.

TINGLING SENSATION OF HANDS AND FEET

My hands and feet were always cold, and I experienced numbness with a tingling sensation on my fingers and toes. I always wore socks and gloves to keep them warm. At work I would always sit by the radiators and never took off my jumper. My colleagues wondered why I was always cold and constantly asked me questions. At the time I did not have an explanation except for that I was feeling unwell.

PAINFUL LEG CRAMPS

I experienced painful leg cramps walking long distances, standing for long periods or in a resting position with my legs bent. The most painful leg cramps occurred during the night while I was sleeping especially when my legs were in a bent position. The mornings were no exception when stretching out of bed. I used to cry out in pain, holding my leg like a child. It was not a pleasant experience.

HEADACHES

I usually do not have headaches but started to experience a lot more headaches. Sometimes they were light, and I could cope without any medication, but others became more pounding and uncomfortable to bear. I am not a lover of medication and would always avoid it where possible for fear of becoming dependent. Lying down in a less noisy environment and having plenty of rest without any electronic gadgets helped.

HEAVY PERIODS

My periods were irregular, very heavy with clots and often painful with cramps. I was always in a lot of discomfort with mood swings during this time of the month and never used to look forward to it. I only wore dark coloured clothing to prevent any embarrassment from blood stains. I called it my 'nightmare times'.

All the symptoms that I have highlighted are from my own personal experience and how I felt. There are many other symptoms of Iron Deficiency Anaemia and remember that every person is different and may have a different experience from me. If you think that you may be experiencing any of the above symptoms persistently then I would strongly advise you to talk to your clinician who may be able to help you. Don't be like me, get it checked out.

PART 1

BOOSTING BREAKFAST

"No one would ever mistake me for an expert on engines, but I know one thing: they don't work without fuel. Our bodies are the same way, which is why I'm passionate about breakfast – especially when it involves passion fruit. And blueberries, And raspberries, some sliced banana and maybe a sprig or two of fresh mint. (And don't forget the bread – you know I love my bread! For breakfast, my preference is multigrain, double toasted."

Oprah

Like Oprah. I love and enjoy having breakfast. It's a must for me because it sets me off in the mornings with lots of energy to keep me going until lunchtime. This also means that I am not tempted to reach out for the less healthy snacks when at work or out and about shopping. Planet earth is blessed with an abundant variety of foods that can be cooked using different tasty methods. What anyone chooses to have as their first meal of the day will usually depend on their lifestyle, culture, taste and many other factors. I grew up in a very loving and caring home in Africa (Cameroon) where breakfast was always served on the table and at the time it was not always a light meal in comparison to most European breakfasts of cereals or toast. I am talking about having mammoth portions of fried ripe plantains or homemade potatoes chips with spicy omelette or scrambled eggs. On some occasions breakfast was left over dinner from the previous day and I am sure most people of

African descent will identify with this. Now that I am living in the United Kingdom I have adapted the culture of keeping it light that is, toast, cornflakes with fruits all weekdays and a cooked breakfast popularly known as 'English breakfast' on my chill-out weekends. The importance of having breakfast became more real to me when I was diagnosed with iron deficiency anaemia (IDA) because it was important to start my day with an iron boosting breakfast such as cereals which are packed with fortified iron. I will share with you some of my favourite breakfast foods and recipes that helped to raise my iron levels.

Cereals

Most breakfast cereals have added iron and my favourite are those which are high in fibre and low in sugar taken with reduced fat milk, sweetener, honey or molasses. I also add a teaspoon of any of these iron-boosters, natural wheat germ, spirulina or maca root powder, a hand full of sultanas, mixed dried fruits or sunflower seeds/mixed seeds. If adding dried fruits, then leave out the sweetener otherwise it may become too sweet.

MY HEALTHY CHOICES -For quantity refer to the individual packets for recommended intake.

Porridge oats
Bran flakes
All Bran
Cornflakes
Muesli
Weetabix biscuits
Shredded wheat biscuit
Fruit 'N' Fibre

Seasonal Fresh Fruits with Natural Yoghurt

INGREDIENTS

1 banana
2 sweet and crispy apples, any
2 ripe and crunchy pears, any
2 Kiwis, ripe and firm
½ lemon, juiced
2-3 tablespoon natural or Greek yoghurt
Drizzle of clear runny honey or molasses
a small handful of sunflower seeds or mixed seeds
1 tablespoon natural wheat germ for dusting

METHOD

1. Wash, core and remove any dark bits from the apples and pears leaving the skin. Cut neatly into bite size chunks. Peel, slice and add banana and kiwi fruits.

2. Place all the fruits in a deep clean bowl and squeeze over the juice from half a lemon to prevent the apples and pears from discolouring. Stir gently with a wooden spoon to coat.

3. Divide the fruits into individual small bowls and top with enough natural yogurt or if you desire you can mix the fruit and yoghurt together.

4. Sprinkle generously with sunflower seeds and drizzle with honey.

5. Dust lightly with natural wheatgerm. Serve immediately or leave in the refrigerator until when needed.

SUGGESTION

Any fruits of choice that is in season can be used. Try mixing other varieties of fruits (tin or fresh) to get a different taste, flavour and colour.

In the winter periods I warm the fruits in the microwave for one minute before eating. You don't have too. It's just my way of keeping warm.

Lovely Apple Banana and Prune Smoothie

INGREDIENTS

2sweet and crispy apples, cored and deseeded
a portion of tin pitted prunes in juice
1 ripe banana
2tablespoons natural or Greek yoghurt
1 teaspoon clear honey or molasses
Drizzle of fresh lemon juice
1 tablespoon natural wheat germ or spirulina powder
1 tall size glass of cold water

METHOD

1. Wash apples and thoroughly, removing any bad bits and cut into chunks. Peel the banana, slice and place all the fruits in an electric food processor or smoothie maker.

2. Add the cold water, wheat-germ, natural yoghurt, honey, lemon juice and blend until well incorporated. Mixture should be creamy in consistency or how you may prefer it by adding a bit more water.

3. Pour into individual glasses and serve immediately or refrigerate for up to one day.

SUGGESTION

Any fruit combination (fresh or tin) can be used for this recipe. Use whatever is available in your fruit bowl or store cupboard

Simply Fruit & Veg Smoothie

INGREDIENTS

1 ripe banana, sliced
1 apple or pear, washed and sliced
1 large carrot washed and sliced
a handful of spinach leaves or kale
½ cucumber
1 tablespoon fresh lemon juice
1 teaspoon clear honey or molasses
1 tablespoon natural wheatgerm or spirulina powder
2 table spoons natural or Greek yoghurt
Sufficient cold water to blend

METHOD

1. Combine the fruits, vegetables, lemon juice, honey, wheatgerm, yoghurt into a blender or smoothie maker. Add sufficient cold water and blend until well combined. Consistency should be how you prefer it. Add more water as desired.

2. Pour into individual glasses and serve or keep in the fridge until needed.

SUGGESTION

Any fruits and vegetables in season and high in iron can be used for this recipe.

Toasted Crumpets with Stewed berries

INGREDIENTS

4 crumpets
1x 250gpunnet strawberry, washed and drained
1 x 250g punnet raspberries, washed and drained
1 x 150g punnet blueberries, washed and drained
Drizzle of lemon juice or white wine vinegar
1 teaspoon clear honey or golden syrup
½ teaspoon ground nutmeg or cinnamon for flavour
2 tablespoon Greek yoghurt for serving
2 tablespoon natural wheat germ for sprinkling

METHOD

1. Dry fry the berries in a non-stick sauce pan on medium heat without oil or water. Fruits will cook slowly in their own juice. Keep an eye on the heat to prevent the fruits from drying out and burning.

2. Add the nutmeg, lemon juice and honey. Stir with a wooden spoon to combine.

3. Simmer the fruits until softened and starts to caramelise but not burnt. Remove it from the heat and set aside. The Consistency of the sauce should be slightly runny. If not, you may sprinkle a small amount of water before taking it off from the heat.

4. Toast the crumpets to desired likeness and place on individual serving plates.

5. Spoon sufficient amounts of stewed fruits on top of each crumpet and serve with a portion of Greek yoghurt. Sprinkle with natural wheat germ and serve. Enjoy!

SUGGESTION

Try using other types of fresh, frozen or tinned fruits of your choice. You may use other combination of berries

Wholemeal Bread with Crunchy Peanut Butter & Banana

INGREDIENTS

4 thick slices of wholemeal bread toasted
2-3 teaspoons crunchy peanut butter
2 ripe and firm bananas
1 tablespoon sunflower seeds or mixed seeds
Sprinkle of spirulina powder or natural wheat germ

METHOD

1. Toast the bread slices to desired likeness. Divide the peanut butter between the four slices of toast and spread evenly using a table knife.

2. Thinly slice the bananas and pile neatly on top of each toast.

3. Sprinkle with sunflower seeds and a dusting of spirulina powder. Serve and enjoy.

SUGGESTION

Wholemeal rolls, Ryvita, bagel, muffin, high protein bread or any other healthy bread options of choice can be used. If you use seeded bread you would not need to add extra sunflower seeds but if you prefer it very seedy why not?

If you do have an allergic reaction to nuts then leave out the peanut butter and use other nut free alternatives such as soft cheese, hummus, cottage cheese, jam/marmalade, butter

African-Style Spicy Hot Scrambled Egg with Kale

INGREDIENTS

4-6 eggs
a large handful of curly kale, chopped
3-4medium size fresh tomato, chopped
1 medium-size onions, peeled and finely chopped
a sprinkle of Maggi sauce all-purpose liquid seasoning
Salt to taste
½ teaspoon hot crushed chillies
1 teaspoon dried mixed herbs
2 tablespoons vegetable oil

METHOD

1. Break the eggs into a clean shallow bowl. Season to taste with salt, Maggi seasoning sauce, mix herbs and chillies. Whisk to combined and set aside. You can use a milder alternative of chillies if you are not a fan of spicy hot food.

2. In a non-stick fry pan heat the vegetable oil over medium heat and fry the onions, kale and tomatoes for approximately 2-3 minutes to soften. Stir constantly to prevent it from burning.

3. Carefully pour in the egg mixture from a close height and cook slowly on medium heat. When it starts to set at the bottom gently scatter the eggs with a fork or spatula. Adjust heat as needed. Stir constantly until cooked evenly and well done with no runny bits. Serve warm.

SUGGESTION

Baby spinach leaves, sardines or any other tin fish are also good iron boosting alternatives.

Gracious Pancakes
with Dark Cocoa Powder

INGREDIENTS

400g all-purpose flour
400ml fresh or pasteurised milk
150g castor or granulated sugar
1 tablespoon dark cocoa powder
½ teaspoon grated or ground nutmeg for flavour
Pinch of salt
2 eggs, beaten
Juice from half a lemon, no seeds
1 tablespoon sunflower oil plus extra for frying
200- 250ml cold water
Drizzle of chocolate sauce, honey or golden syrup for serving

METHOD

1. Combine all the dry ingredients in a medium size clean bowl and stir with a hand whisk until well combined.

2. Make a well in the centre and carefully add in all the wet ingredients and whisk until fully incorporated. The batter should be smooth, light and of a semi-runny consistency with no lumps. You can use a food processor or electric whisk at this stage as it saves time and energy, but I prefer to give my arm a good workout using the manual whisk.

3. Heat a good size heavy base frying pan on medium heat and coat lightly with oil. Carefully pour a ladleful of the batter into the frying pan. Hold the handle firmly and lift the pan up slightly and swirl gently in all directions to cover the base of the pan thinly. Check and adjust the heat accordingly to prevent burning.

4. Fry on moderate heat until it starts to get firm on one side and bubbles start to appear on the top of the pancake. Flip over to the other side and cook for approximately two minutes until evenly brown and cooked through. Taste the first batch and adjust batter as required. I say so because a few people who have tried out this recipe added more sugar – they confessed to having a sweet tooth.

5. Slide on to a clean plate and repeat the process with the remaining batter until the mixture is all used up.

6. Fold each pancake in halve or to desired shape. Serve warm with a drizzle of chocolate sauce or any other sauce you may prefer or have in your cupboard.

SUGGESTION

2 ripe bananas (smoothly mashed) are a good alternative to cocoa powder

Tasty French Baguette with Avocado

INGREDIENTS

1 long French baguette, fresh, soft and evenly brown
2 ripe and firm avocados, peeled, stone removed and roughly chopped
2 ripe and firm salad tomatoes, thinly sliced
1 teaspoon ground black pepper
1 tablespoon butter for extra flavour
A large handful of baby spinach for layering
a handful of mixed seeds for sprinkling

METHOD

1. Carefully cut and Split open the baguette into two halves across the middle and place on a clean board with the cut side up. Spread both halves evenly with butter. Put the top halve aside for later.

2. Layer the bottom half of the baguette with baby leaves spinach to look like a blanket and neatly place the sliced tomatoes to cover the full length of the baguette.

3. Top generously with chopped avocado and sprinkle with mixed seeds. sprinkle lightly with ground black pepper. Avocados can taste bland, but a light sprinkle of salt will make it enjoyable.

4. Replace the buttered half of the baguette on top and gently press down firmly to close. Cut into halves. Serve on individual plates.

SUGGESTION

Cream cheese is also a good alternative if you do not have avocado. Try using other varieties of leafy salads. I have also tried using chopped sweet red pepper mixed with the avocado and it was delicious.

Curried Bake Beans on Toast

INGREDIENTS

4-6 thick slices of wholemeal bread for serving
2 x 410g can bake beans in tomato sauce
1 small onion, finely chopped
1 red or green pepper, deseeded and finely chopped
½ level tea spoon curry powder
½ teaspoon garam masala
1 teaspoon dried mixed herbs
½ tea spoon crushed hot chillies (optional)
Sprinkle of all-purpose Maggi sauce liquid seasoning
1 teaspoon butter to spread on toast (optional)
1 tablespoon cooking oil

METHOD

1. Heat the oil in non-stick medium size sauce pan over low heat. Add in the chopped onions, green pepper and cook slowly until just soft (if you are tearful when handling onions, you can use spring onions)

2. Pour in the beans from the can and season to taste with a sprinkling of Maggi sauce seasoning, mixed dried herbs, curry powder, garam masala and chillies.

3. Stir to mix and simmer on low heat until completely warmed through.

4. Toast the slices of bread to desire likeness and spread lightly with butter.

5. Place on individual serving plates and carefully spoon the beans equally over each slice of toast. Serve warm.

SUGGESTION

A handful of sliced mushrooms can also be added to the bake beans. If this is to be done, it should be fried together with the onions.

So-Simple Eggy Bread with Wheat Germ

INGREDIENTS

8-10 thick slices of wholemeal bread. Cut into halves
6-8 eggs
salt to taste
Pinch of chilli powder
1 teaspoon dried mixed herbs
½ teaspoon ground nutmeg
Sprinkle of Maggi sauce seasoning
2-4 teaspoon natural wheat germ, save some for sprinkling
Sufficient vegetable Oil for frying

METHOD

1. Crack the eggs into a medium size shallow bowl and beat well using a fork or balloon whisk. Season to taste with salt, nutmeg, chilli powder, mixed herbs and a light sprinkle of Maggi seasoning sauce. Add a two teaspoon of natural wheatgerm and Continue to beat until thoroughly combined and fluffy.

2. Heat sufficient oil in a non-stick frying pan over medium heat without allowing it to smoke. Using clean hands take each slice of bread and dunk carefully into the egg mixture to coat on both sides then gently slide into the oil. Do the same for a few more slices making sure you do not overload the frying pan.

3. Monitor the heat and cook until bread is cooked and golden brown on both sides with no soggy areas. Transfer onto a clean serving plate and repeat the process until bread is finished. If you run out of egg mixture, just add one more egg and season lightly to finish off. If you run out of bread just add a few more slices. When done pile neatly on a plate and sprinkle with natural wheat germ. Serve warm.

SUGGESTION

You can use any other type of bread available. It is better to use bread that has been a few days old but still in date because it will hold better when soaked in the egg mixture.

Fruity Breakfast Muffins

INGREDIENTS

250g plain flour
100g castor sugar
150g raisins or dried mix fruits
¼ teaspoon salt
1 teaspoon ground cinnamon or nutmeg
2 teaspoon baking powder
¼ teaspoon bicarbonate of soda
2 ripe bananas
2 eggs
Juice from ½ a lemon
125g vegetable or sunflower oil
3 tablespoon natural yoghurt or fresh milk
a handful of porridge oats for topping

METHOD

1. Preheat the oven and line a regular size muffin tray with paper cases. You may need to line an extra muffin tray for any surplus.

2. In a good size deep clean bowl mix all the dry ingredients together including the dried fruits and stir with a wooden spoon to combine. Leave aside.

3. In another bowl mash up the bananas with a fork or potato masher to a slightly lumpy texture.

4. Combine the dry and wet ingredients together and stir gently using a spatula to mix. The batter should be of a dropping consistency and drop of the spoon with ease when held upright with a steady hand. A tablespoon of milk or natural yoghurt can be added as desired to obtain the desired consistency if not reached.

5. Using an ice cream scoop neatly fill each muffin case to the half full mark to avoid over spilling and loss of shape when cooking.

6. Lightly sprinkle porridge oats over the top and place in the middle of a preheated oven for 20-25 minutes on medium heat until well risen and golden. Check for doneness by inserting a skewer into the middle. If it comes out wet, then it will need to stay in the oven for a few more minutes until it is perfectly ready.

7. Leave to cool on the rack. Serve when needed.

SUGGESTION

Different variety or a combination of fruits can be used as alternatives to bananas

PART 2

UPLIFTING LIGHT LUNCHES

"I believe in stopping work and eating lunch"

L'Wren Scott

My mornings are usually very busy and being that active saw my energy levels dropped visibly by midday. This often made me restless and irritable with loss of concentration. It is interesting to see how the body has its own unique way of speaking to us and giving clear instructions that can be hard to ignore such as hunger. In my case when I start to feel hungry my attention gets diverted to the food contents in my pack lunch bag. Preparing and taking healthy pack lunches to work saves me a few pounds in my pocket and keeps my waistline in check. I am sure you will agree with me that most canteen or restaurant foods are hardly on the healthy side and can be expensive in the long term. These recipes can be prepared in advance or put together at work using the microwave. It's simple and easy.

Vibrant Jacket Potato with Cheese

INGREDIENTS

2-4 medium size baking potatoes
150g-200g grated cheddar cheese
1-2 medium size carrot, washed and grated
1green pepper, deseeded and chopped
Pinch of salt and black pepper
a small amount of cooking oil for extra flavour on potatoes (optional)
1 teaspoon butter for serving (optional)
a handful of washed baby leaf spinach for serving

METHOD

1. Thoroughly scrub the potatoes removing any bad bits. Rub lightly with a small amount of cooking oil for extra flavour and shine.

2. Place on a lined baking tray and cook in the middle of a hot oven for an hour checking and turning sides at intervals until the potatoes are crispy on the outside, soft and tender when prodded with a skewer or pointed knife.

3. Whilst the potatoes are cooking combine the cheese, carrots and green peppers in a bowl. Stir to mix.

4. When potatoes are cooked, remove and leave to the side for a few minutes to let off some of the steam because it can be very hot to handle straight from the oven.

5. When cool carefully split open each potato in the middle with a knife sprinkle lightly with salt and black pepper. Lightly spread both sides with butter if desire.

6. Spoon sufficient amount of the cheese and vegetable mixture onto each potato. If you prefer you can put the

potatoes back in the oven or microwave for approximately 1-2 minutes to melt the cheese.

7. Serve on a bed of baby spinach leaves.

SUGGESTION

You can use different combinations of fillings of your choice. Potatoes can also be cooked in the microwave if you are short of time. This is one of my simple and easy recipes and a work favourite. I usually prepare all the ingredients overnight for work the next morning.

Mind-Blowing Coleslaw

INGREDIENTS

¼ white cabbage, finely shredded

¼ red cabbage, finely shredded

1 red or green pepper, seeds removed and thinly diced

2 celery stalks, washed and thinly chopped

4 spring onions, washed, trimmed and finely chopped

a handful of curly kale, finely chopped

4-6 carrots, washed and grated

a handful of mixed dried fruits or currants

For Dressing

2 tablespoons mayonnaise

4-6 tablespoon natural yoghurt

1 teaspoon mustard

Pinch of salt and black pepper

Juice from 1 lemon, no seeds

2 tablespoon olive oil

2 tablespoon clear honey or golden syrup

2 tablespoon good drinking dry white wine or white wine vinegar (optional)

METHOD

1. Combine all the vegetables and dried fruits in a large deep bowl and mix well with a wooden spoon. Set aside

2. In a separate bowl prepare the dressing by whisking all the ingredients together until smooth and well blended.

3. Gently pour the dressing over the coleslaw mixture and stir to coat. Add more dressing as desire if you like it creamy. Taste and adjust seasoning as require.

4. Cover and chill in the fridge until ready to serve.

SUGGESTION

Sun dried prunes, crispy apples or pineapple chunks are good alternatives to currants.

Jazzed-Up Instant Noodles

INGREDIENTS

3 x 108g packets instant noodles
1 x 400g can red kidney beans, rinsed and drained
Portion of shredded cooked chicken or beef
1 onions, peeled and sliced
1 large handful of mixed vegetables
Pinch of hot chilli pepper powder (optional)
2 Maggi or Knorr cube all-purpose seasoning, crushed
½ teaspoon curry powder
1 teaspoon dried mixed herbs
Salt to taste

METHOD

1. Empty the contents of the noodle packets into a saucepan with sufficient boiling water without the sachet of flavouring that comes with it. (I do not usethe sachet flavouring because of the taste it leaves in the mouth). You may use it if you prefer but you will have to reduce the quantity of salt and seasoning you use.

2. Add the vegetables, beans and shredded chicken. Season to taste with all the spices. Cover to cook on moderate heat for 10- 15 minutes stirring at intervals to allow all the flavours to come together.

3. Noodles should be cooked to al-dente and vegetables crunchy. Do not allow the water to run dry. Serve warm.

SUGGESTION

Noodles can also be cooked in the microwave. Any vegetables or pre-cooked pulses or lentils of choice can be used. This recipe makes a good pack lunch for work. I take all the ingredients in a microwaveable container and just add water at work and leave the rest to the 'ping' machine.

Scrumptious Quinoa with Tuna Salad

INGREDIENTS

400g quinoa grains, uncooked
1x400g can chickpeas, drained
2-4 spring onions, trimmed and finely chopped
1 stalk celery sticks, washed and finely chopped
1 red or green pepper deseeded and thinly diced
a handful of pitted olives, green or black
I x 160g can tuna in water, drained
1 x 200g packet baby spinach leaves, for serving

For the Dressing

4-6 tablespoon olive oil
1 teaspoon mild mustard
Juice from ½ lemon, without seeds
Pinch of salt and black pepper
1 tablespoon runny honey or golden syrup

METHOD

1. Cook the quinoa grains according to the instructions on the packet. Transfer into a medium size bowl and leave aside to cool.

2. Whisk all the ingredients for the dressing in a deep bowl until well combined or you can shake them in a jar with lid until emulsified. Leave in the fridge.

3. When the grains are cool add in all the vegetables and tuna. Pour sufficient dressing over the salad and mix gently with a wooden spoon to coat. Do not drench the salad because it will become soggy. Serve on a bed of baby spinach leaves. Serve at once or store in the fridge for when needed.

SUGGESTION

Salmon, sardines, smoked mackerel fillets or any oily fish can also be used in place of tuna. You can also use other varieties of vegetables

Enchanting salad with Prawns

INGREDIENTS

1 green sweet pepper, seeds removed and sliced
1 yellow sweet pepper, seeds removed and sliced
3-pointed chilli pepper, chopped with seeds
a handful of radish, sliced
¼ cucumber, sliced
1 x 198g can sweet corn, drained
1 x 300g can marrowfat peas, drained
1 x 250 packet cooked prawns
1-2 balls of beetroot, sliced or quartered
Pinch of salt and black pepper

For the Dressing

1 tablespoon mayonnaise, for dressing
2-3 tablespoon natural yoghurt
Juice from ½ a lemon, no seeds
1 teaspoon honey or golden syrup
1 teaspoon spirulina or natural wheat germ
Drizzle of olive oil

METHOD

1. Put all the salad vegetables into a medium size bowl. Leave out the beetroot to add just before serving to prevent discolouring. Season with salt and black pepper. Toss to mix.

2. Add the prawns and drizzle over the dressing as required. Stir thoroughly with a wooden spoon to mix.

3. Scatter the beetroot pieces over the salad and serve at once or chill in the fridge until when needed.

SUGGESTION

You may use other variety of vegetables and substitute the prawns for what you may prefer

Delicious Lentils and Butternut Squash Soup

INGREDIENTS

400g uncooked lentils, red or green
½ butternut squash, peeled and sliced
1 stalk of celery, roughly chopped
I onions, peeled and chopped
2 Maggi or Knorr all-purpose seasoning cubes, crushed
1 teaspoon dried mixed herbs
½ teaspoon crushed hot peppers (optional)
1 level teaspoon curry powder
1 small piece of ginger, grated
Salt to taste

METHOD

1. Soak lentils in sufficient cold water for 1-2 hours then boil until tender. check occasionally. To check if cooked pick up a few grains with a spoon and bite into it. Drain when done.

2. Pour sufficient boiling water from a kettle into a non-stick good size pot with lid. Add the butternut squash, lentils, onions and celery.

3. Season with salt, Maggi cubes, ginger, curry powder, mix herbs and chillies.

4. Simmer for 15- 20 minutes on medium heat stirring occasionally until spices and flavours come together and butternut squash cooked. Taste and adjust seasoning as desire.

5. When cooked remove from the heat and leave aside until cool enough to blend using an electric hand-held blender. Consistency may be how you prefer it. (I prefer mine with

chewy bits). If using a cylinder blender leave soup to be completely cool to avoid any explosion.

6. Stir with a wooden spoon to mix after blending. Soup can be placed back on low heat for 3-5 minutes before serving. You may wish to skip this part and serve once blended.

SUGGESTION

Potatoes are a tasty alternative to butternut squash.

Glorious Green Salad with Avocado & Pumpkin Seeds

INGREDIENTS

1 x 200g packet ready washed baby leaf spinach
¼ wedge lettuce leaves, washed, drain and roughly torn
1 x 100g bag rocket leaves
3-6 spring onions, trimmed and chopped
1 large green pepper, seeds removed and thinly sliced
a handful of green pumpkin seeds, lightly toasted
1-2 ripe and firm avocado, peeled stoned and sliced
Pinch of salt and ground black

For the Dressing

4-6 tablespoon olive oil
1 teaspoon mustard
2 tablespoon clear honey
2 tablespoon dry white wine or white wine vinegar
Juice from 1 lemon, no seeds
Pinch of salt and black pepper
1 teaspoon spirulina powder plus extra for sprinkling

METHOD

1. Place all the green vegetables in a clean deep bowl and toss to mix.

2. Pile neatly onto a serving platter. Place the sliced avocado decoratively and sprinkle generously with toasted pumpkin seeds.

3. Prepare the dressing by whisking all ingredients together until well combined. Drizzle over salad with a sprinkle of spirulina and serve.

SUGGESTION

You may use any combination of green leafy salad or vegetables you prefer

Broccoli Curly Kale and Carrot Soup

INGREDIENTS

1 branch of broccoli florets, cut into chunks
a handful of curly kale
3 medium size carrots. Washed and sliced
1 onion, peeled and chopped
2 Maggi or Knorr all-purpose seasoning cube, crushed
1 teaspoon curry powder
2-4 garlic cloves, peeled &chopped
½ scotch bonnet pepper, chopped
Salt to taste

METHOD

1. Wash all the vegetables thoroughly. Chop and put in a pot with sufficient water.

6. Season to taste with all the spices and cover to cook until vegetables are tender but not mushy. You may add the scotch bonnet with or without seeds depending on how hot you like.

2. When done leave to cool and then blend using an electric hand blender or food processor into a semi smooth puree. If you are using a blender with a cylinder bowl, ensure soup is completely cool to avoid explosion.

7. This soup may not look pretty in appearance, but it is a delicious iron booster and one of my favourites.

SUGGESTION

You may use other combination of iron boosting vegetables for this recipe.

Pitta Bread Pockets with Chicken Salad

INGREDIENTS

2-4 whole meal pitta bread
2 large portion of cooked chicken breast, Shredded
a handful of currants
1 red or green pepper, deseeded and sliced into strips
2 ripe and firm salad tomatoes, thinly sliced
a handful of baby leaf spinach for layering

For the dressing

3-4 tablespoon natural yoghurt
1 tablespoon mayonnaise
1teaspoon mild mustard
1 teaspoon lemon juice
Drizzle of vegetable or olive oil
Pinch of salt and black pepper

METHOD

1. In a clean bowl combine the shredded chicken, currants, red peppers and mix with a wooden spoon. Whisk all the ingredients for the dressing together and pour over the chicken mixture. Stir to coat.

2. Warm the pitta bread in a toaster on low level heat to ensure it remains soft and flexible to handle. Leave for a few minutes to cool. Carefully make a slit alongside with a knife. Be careful not to completely cut open the pitta bread.

3. Neatly place the spinach leaves and tomato slices onto the pitta pockets and spoon in sufficient amounts of the chicken mixture. Serve and enjoy.

SUGGESTION

Pitta pockets can be filled with whatever you desire. Try using different types of salad

Sizzling Oven Cooked Vegetables with smoked Mackerel Fillets

INGREDIENTS

1 branch of broccoli, stalk removed and cut into chunks
1 large bulb of cauliflower florets cut into chunks
2 x 170g packet smoked mackerel fillets
4-6 carrots, sliced into chunks
2 onions, peeled and quartered
1leeks, washed and sliced
2-3 celery stalk, washed and sliced
4-6 medium size potato, quartered with skin
2 x 400g cans plum or chopped tomato
2-3Maggi or Knorr all-purpose seasoning cubes, crushed
1 teaspoon hot crushed chilli1 teaspoon curry powder
1 teaspoon dried mixed herbs
4-6 garlic cloves, roughly chopped
1 small piece root ginger, sliced
Salt to taste
3-4 tablespoon cooking oil

METHOD

1. Arrange all vegetables as desire in a good size oven proof dish.

2. Season with salt, chillies, Maggi cubes, curry powder, mixed herbs, ginger and garlic. Stir with a wooden spoon for spices to blend together. Place the mackerel fillets on top of the vegetables. You can shred the mackerel fillets into big pieces and mix it in if you desire.

3. Pour over the plum tomato with juice and drizzle all over with cooking oil.

4. Lift and shake the dish gently from side to side to ensure the tomato juice is evenly distributed.

5. Cover with foil and cook in the oven on moderate heat for 20-30 minutes until vegetables are tender but crunchy and the juice has slightly reduced.

6. Remove from heat and serve.

SUGGESTION

Any iron rich vegetables, meat or fish products you have in your fridge or storage can also be used as alternatives.

French Stick Pizza

INGREDIENTS

1 long and fresh French stick
4 tablespoon passata or ketchup
125g pack mozzarella cheese, sliced
300g grated cheddar cheese
2 green peppers, deseeded and diced
1 x 300g can sweet corn, drained
2 tablespoon olive oil
Pinch of salt and black pepper

METHOD

1. Cut the French stick into four halves and each halve lengthwise.

2. Brush each halve with olive oil and spread evenly with passata. Cover with mozzarella and cheddar cheese. Top with diced sweet pepper and sweetcorn.

3. Season with salt and black pepper. Place bread halves on a lined oven tray and cook in the oven on moderate heat for 10-15 minutes or until cheese has melted and vegetables tender. Serve when cool. Enjoy!

SUGGESTION

Other varieties of vegetables or cheese can be used. Make this recipe exciting and fun.

Mixed Root Vegetable Salad

INGREDIENTS

3-6 medium size potatoes
2 parsnips
¾ wedge Swede
3 carrots
2 small pointed hot chillies, chopped.
4hard-boiledeggs cut into quarters
4 spring onions or1 small red onion, chopped
a handful of mixed seeds for sprinkling
salt and black pepper to taste
50g grated cheddar cheese for extra richness (optional)
1 x 200g bag baby spinach leaves for serving

For the dressing

3-4 tablespoon natural yoghurt
2 tablespoon cooking oil
1 tablespoon lemon juice
1 tablespoon honey
2 tablespoon natural wheat germ
1 teaspoon mustard

METHOD

1. Wash, peel and cut all vegetables into small cubes. Boil in lightly salted water until tender but holding its shape. Set aside to cool. Vegetables should be crunchy to bite.

2. Put vegetables in a deep bowl and sprinkle with black pepper. Add in the spring onions, eggs, chillies and sunflower seeds. Pour over sufficient dressing without

drenching the vegetables. Stir carefully with a wooden spoon taking care not to mash up vegetables.

3. Prepare the dressing by whisking together all the ingredients until well combined. Pour over sufficient dressing without drenching the vegetables. Stir carefully with a wooden spoon taking care not to mash up vegetables.

4. Sprinkle with grated cheese and garnish with chopped green peppers. Serve on a bed of baby leave spinach or keep in the fridge for when needed.

SUGGESTION

You may use other types of root vegetables for this recipe. Use a variety of colours and texture to make it interesting.

PART 3

HEARTY MAIN MEALS

"The most essential part of my day is a proper dinner"

Rachael Ray

The end of a busy day always brings a smile to me knowing that dinner time is never far away. For me, it's always an opportunity for all my family to come together on the table and share stories and experiences of the day. This has been a long running tradition in my family – a valuable time together.

Jollof Rice with Sardines and Chickpeas

INGREDIENTS

500g basmati rice or any good quality long grain rice, uncooked
2 x 400g can chopped tomatoes
1 large onions, peeled and sliced
4-6 large garlic cloves, peeled and crushed
1 medium size ginger, peeled and grated
1 size scotch bonnet pepper, crushed with or without seeds (optional)
1 teaspoon curry powder
3-4 Maggi cube all-purpose seasoning, crushed
1 teaspoon dried mixed herbs
Salt to taste
1 x 400g can chickpeas, drained
4 medium size carrots, sliced or 200g mixed vegetables
4 x 120g can sardines in tomato sauce
3-4 tablespoon cooking oil
1 green pepper seeds removed and sliced for garnishing

METHOD

1. Combine the tomatoes, onions, garlic, ginger, scotch bonnet into and electric blender and blend until smooth. Set aside.

2. In a large size heavy base pot with lid, heat up the oil on medium heat and pour in the blended mixture as close as possible to the pot and away from you to reduce splashing and sneezing from the blended pepper.

3. At this stage reduce the heat because it may start to spit violently. Stir gently with a wooden spoon and season to taste with salt, Maggi cubes, curry powder and mix herbs. Add two large glasses of water and stir to mix. Cover with

lid to the boil. Slightly increase the heat again to medium and simmer for 3- 5 minutes for flavours and ingredients to come together.

4. Add the rice and stir slowly (most recipes will recommend you to par-boil the rice but the downside of this is that the rice will become too soft, soggy and lose texture) but is fine to wash and drain the rice before cooking to reduce the starch before adding to the sauce.

5. Stir the rice gently with a wooden spoon in a clockwise direction to ensure the grains do not get broken and mashed up. Taste and adjust seasoning as desire. Cover and let it cook for 10 -15 minutes until the water has been soaked up. Throw in the chickpeas, vegetables and sardines in oil and stir to mix. (Do not use too much of the oil from the sardines otherwise the rice would become too oily)

6. Check rice for doneness by biting into a few grains. Add water in small amounts if needed. Continue to cook slowly for a further 15-20 minutes on medium heat checking and stirring lightly at intervals. Keep a close eye on the heat and reduce if necessary so that it does not burn at the bottom. The rice should be cooked to al-dente but tender with grains not sticking tightly together.

7. Reduce the heat to very low when grains are cooked and leave for about 5-10 minutes for any excess water to dry off.

8. When ready serve warm on individual plates and garnish with sliced green peppers.

SUGGESTION

I have not followed the traditional jollof rice recipe to incorporate iron rich ingredients and toned down the spicy hot aspect of this dish. Any leftover meat, chicken, corn beef, prawns or boneless smoked fish fillets can be used for this recipe. Tin mackerel or salmon also taste delicious.

Wheatgerm Coated Sticky Chicken Wings

INGREDIENTS

15-20pieces fresh chicken wings
2 Maggi or Knorr all-purpose seasoning cube, crushed
Pinch of salt to taste
2 cups of natural wheatgerm to coat

For the Sticky Sauce

4 tablespoon tomato ketchup or passata
4 tablespoon brown sauce
4 tablespoon sweet chilli sauce
4 tablespoon dark soy sauce
4tablespoon clear honey or golden syrup
4 tablespoon balsamic vinegar or lemon juice
3 tablespoon cooking oil

METHOD

1. Wash chicken wings thoroughly and remove any hidden feathers. Place in a bowl and season with salt and Maggi all-purpose seasoning.

2. Place on a lightly greased foiled-lined roasting tray and place in a preheated oven on moderate heat to cook until half done. Remove from the heat and set aside.

3. Meanwhile mix all the ingredients for the sticky sauce in a small pot and bring to simmer until the sauce becomes semi thick in consistency. Stir frequently but gently to prevent the sauce from burning and sticking to the bottom.

4. Remove from the heat and carefully dunk small batches of chicken wings into the sticky sauce and stir to coat evenly.

Transfer back onto the roasting tray and repeat process until chicken wings are finished.

5. Place in the oven and continue to cook on medium heat until done. Check and turn sides as required to allow all sides to cook evenly and prevent burning. When cooked coat well with sufficient natural wheat germ and put back into the oven for 3-5 minutes to seal. That way the wheatgerm coating does not burn but have a golden colour and a lovely feel in the mouth. Serve warm.

SUGGESTION

Spare ribs or any other meat of choice can be used in place of wings. Sesame seeds are also good for coating.

Chickpeas Curry

INGREDIENTS

3 x 400g tin chickpeas, drained
1 x 400ml tin coconut milk
1 large onions, chopped
2-4 Maggi cubes or stock cubes, crushed
Ginger and garlic, chopped
Salt and chilli flakes to taste
1 teaspoon curry powder
1 teaspoon garam masala
1 teaspoon ground coriander
2 tablespoon cooking oil

METHOD

1. Heat the oil on medium heat in a non-stick pot. Fry in the onions, ginger, garlic and curry spices and stir for a few seconds.

2. Pour in the coconut milk and season with curry spices, Maggi cubes, salt and chilli to taste.

3. Add in the chickpeas, stir to mix, cover and cook until sauce becomes semi-thick in consistency and flavours well combined. Taste and adjust seasoning as required. You may add a bit of water if require. When done, serve with whatever you desire.

SUGGESTION

This curry is delicious served with any type of flat bread

Mix Bean Curry

INGREDIENTS

1 x 400g can red kidney beans, drained
1 x 400g can crab eye beans, drained
1 x 400g can black eye beans
4-6 tablespoon passata
1x349 packet firm tofu, cut into cubes
1 large onions, peeled and chopped
4 garlic cloves, peeled and crushed
1 small ginger, peeled and grated
4 garlic cloves, peeled and crushed
½ teaspoon crushed chillies
½ teaspoon ground cumin
½ teaspoon ground coriander
½ teaspoon ground garam masala
½ teaspoon curry powder
2-4Maggi cube all-purpose seasoning, crushed
Salt to taste
3 tablespoon cooking oil

METHOD

1. Heat the oil on medium heating a good size pot with lid. Add the onions, ginger and garlic and sweat for approximately one-minute stirring constantly.

2. Add in all the curry spices and fry for approximately one minute to let off the aroma. At this stage reduce the heat to prevent it from burning. Pour in the passata, tofu, beans. Stir and add 1-2 small cups of water.

3. Season to taste with the remaining ingredients. Increase the heat slightly and bring to the boil for 15-20 minutes until

the sauce becomes semi thick in consistency and flavours well infused. Serve warm.

SUGGESTION

Try combining other types of beans for this recipe.

Easy Fried Rice with Shrimps

INGREDIENTS

500g basmati or long grain rice, cooked
200g frozen peas, defrosted
1 onion, peeled and sliced
1 small piece root ginger, peeled and grated
2-4 garlic cloves. peeled and crushed
Salt and crushed chillies to taste
Sprinkle of Maggi all-purpose seasoning sauce
2 Maggi or Knorr all-purpose seasoning cube, crushed
1 x 150g pack of peeled shrimps
½ stalk leeks, washed and thinly sliced
3 tablespoon cooking oil
4-6 stalks of spring onions, washed and chopped for garnish

METHOD

1. Heat the oil on moderate heat. Do not allow it to overheat or it will smoke. Quickly stir in the onions, leeks, ginger and garlic. Add the shrimps and frozen peas and continue to stir for 2-5 minutes to allow vegetables to soften and flavours to combine.

2. Add the cooked rice and mix well to combine. Season to taste with salt, Maggi cubes, crushed chillies and Maggi sauce. Simmer gently on medium heat until vegetables are just tender, and the rice has absorbed all the flavours. Taste and adjust seasoning as desire.

3. Remove from heat garnish with chopped spring onions and serve warm.

SUGGESTION

Any meat or sea food of choice can be used. Use whatever iron-boosting alternative takes your fancy. Let your imagination take control. Leftover rice is also good to use.

Truly Irritable Dry-Fried Ox Liver

INGREDIENTS

600g fresh ox liver, washed, drained and thinly sliced
3-6 tablespoon cooking oil
1 large onion, peeled and sliced
2-3 garlic cloves, peeled and chopped
1 thumb size ginger, peeled and grated
2Maggi or Knorr all-purpose seasoning cube, crushed
Salt and crushed chillies to taste
1 green or red or yellow pepper, seeds removed and cut into thin strips for garnish

METHOD

1. Heat the cooking oil on moderate heat in a good size non-stick pot or frying pan. Fry the onions, garlic and ginger together for approximately 10 seconds and then add in the liver pieces. Stir to mix.

2. Season to taste with Maggi cubes, salt and chillies. Increase the heat slightly Stirring constantly to prevent it from burning. Do not cover or add water because it will make the liver lose its taste, texture and flavour. The juice from the liver and the oil will cook the liver nicely. If you find it a little bit too dry, drizzle with a small amount of oil.

3. Check heat and continue to cook and stir until liver is cooked through. Taste and adjust seasoning as desire. Be careful not to overcook the liver or it will taste rubbery. Liver should be moist and succulent. (I prefer it a little bit rare but if you don't then continue to cook for a little bit longer) Remove from heat garnish with green or red peppers and serve.

SUGGESTION

Lamb or chicken liver is a tasty alternative. I like this recipe because liver is not expensive and it's quick to cook.

Aromatic Chicken Curry with Coconut Milk

INGREDIENTS

3-4 tablespoon cooking oil

4-6 chicken portions cut into bite size pieces

1 onion, peeled and chopped

4-6 garlic cloves, peeled and chopped

1 small piece ginger, peeled and grated

1 teaspoon ground cinnamon

1 teaspoon ground coriander

6-8 piece of cloves, finely crushed

1 teaspoon curry powder

1 teaspoon turmeric

2-3 Maggi all-purpose seasoning cubes, crushed

Salt and hot crushed chillies to taste

1 x 400ml can coconut milk

4-6 bay leaves

METHOD

1. Heat oil in a heavy base saucepan. Fry the chicken pieces and cook for 3-5 minutes on moderate heat. Turn regularly to seal and brown on both sides. Remove from heat and set aside.

2. In the same saucepan fry the onions and all the other curry spices and stir until well blended and flavours infused. Carefully pour in the coconut milk and bring to a gentle simmer. Add the chicken pieces and season to taste with salt, Maggi cubes and chillies. Add in the bay leaves.

3. Add 1-2 full cup of boiling water and continue cook on medium heat for 20-30 minutes until chicken is tender and sauce has slightly thickened. Serve warm.

SUGGESTION

Any meat, fish or poultry of choice can be used for this recipe.

Succulent Parcel-Baked Salmon Fillet

INGREDIENTS

2x 270g pack salmon fillet

1-2Maggi or Knorr all-purpose seasoning cubes, crushed

Salt and hot chilli powder to taste

1 teaspoon dried mixed herbs

1 teaspoon all-purpose seasoning

1 large onion, peeled and sliced

1 large green pepper, deseeded and sliced

1-2 tablespoon cooking oil for moisture

METHOD

1. Place the salmon fillets in a bowl and season to taste with all the spices. Rub well to coat on both sides using clean hands. Handle gently to prevent fillet from breaking apart.

2. Transfer on to a sizeable greased foil paper and place the sliced onion and sliced peppers on top of the fish. Drizzle with cooking oil to keep it moist and loosely wrap up in a parcel-like shape. Place on a baking tray and shove in the middle of a hot oven to cook for 20-25 minutes on moderate heat depending on the size of the fillet.

3. Check at intervals by removing from the oven and inserting a knife tip into the thickest part of the fillet and gently pry it open. If the fish separates into flakes, it's done, if not return to the oven for a few more minutes. When done fish should be moist, tasty with some nutritious juices. Delicious.

SUGGESTION

Any fish of choice can be used as an alternative to salmon. Mackerel fillet taste very delicious cooked in the same way

Wow- Factor Spaghetti 'N' Mince

INGREDIENTS

2-3 tablespoon cooking oil

1 x 500g beef mince or any

1 x 500g packet spaghetti, uncooked

2 x 400g can chopped tomato

1 x 400g can kala Chana peas or red kidney beans, drained

2-4 medium size carrots, sliced into small chunks

1 large onions, peeled and chopped

4 garlic cloves, peeled and crushed

1 medium size root ginger, peeled and grated

1 scotch bonnet pepper, chopped with seeds (optional)

2-4 Maggi or Knorr cube all-purpose seasoning

1 teaspoon dried mixed herbs

1 teaspoon curry powder

Salt to taste

150g grated cheddar cheese for serving (Optional)

METHOD

1. Heat vegetable oil in a good size heavy base pot with lid. Fry the onions, ginger and garlic for a few seconds to let off some aroma. Add the mincemeat with the remaining ingredients stir with a wooden spoon for ingredients to combine.

2. Continue to cook on medium heat until the mince beef starts to change in colour. Pour in the chopped tomato, kala Chana peas and carrots. Sprinkle with sufficient salt and pepper to taste. Cover with lid and bring to a gentle simmer. Check and stir at intervals adjusting heat as required. Add a small cup of water if needed.

3. Cook mincemeat until the volume of liquid has slightly reduced and the sauce has a rich and semi thick consistency. Just before the mincemeat is ready boil the spaghetti according to packet instructions and drain.

4. Add the spaghetti to the mincemeat sauce and stir thoroughly to coat. Leave on low heat for 3-5 minutes to warm through and soak in the flavours.

5. Serve warm with a sprinkle of grated cheddar cheese if desire.

SUGGESTION

Any pulse can be used as delicious alternatives.

Flavourful sautéed Spinach with Boiled Green Plantains

INGREDIENTS

3-4 tablespoon cooking oil

6 x 400g bag whole leaf spinach

1 x 300g mushrooms, washed and halved

1 x 27og pack smoked mackerel fillets, shredded

1 large onions, chopped

1 scotch bonnet pepper, chopped (optional)

4 garlic cloves, crushed

1 medium ginger, grated

1 tablespoon powdered crayfish (optional)

2Maggi cube all-purpose seasoning

Salt to taste

4 green plantains for serving

METHOD

1. Heat the oil in a non-stick pot on moderate heat and fry in the onions, ginger and garlic. Stir to prevent it from burning. Add the spinach leaves, mushrooms, mackerel fillets and ground crayfish. Season to taste with salt, Maggi cubes and pepper. Mix well to combine.

2. At this stage reduce the heat to low and cook for approximately 5-10 minutes until spinach has completely wilted and flavours blended. Do not cover to allow some of the excess water to evaporate. Taste and adjust seasoning as required and when cooked remove from the heat, cover with lid and set aside.

3. Meanwhile prepare the green plantains by cutting off both ends leave the skin on, cut in halves and boil in sufficient

water. Plantains should be submerged in water. Cook for 30-40 minutes or until tender and cooked through.

4. When done, drain, remove skin and serve on a plate with spinach.

SUGGESTION

Any other root vegetable or can be used as an alternative to plantains. I use plantain because it is a good source of iron combined with spinach.

Powdered crayfish and plantains can be brought from any African or ethnic supermarket.

Mouth-Watering Beef Casserole

INGREDIENTS

2 x 400g packet diced beef
2 x 400g can chopped tomato
1 large onions, peeled and roughly chopped
1 teaspoon curry powder
2-4 Maggi all-purpose seasoning cubes, crushed
I teaspoon dried mixed herbs
1 small piece root ginger, peeled and chopped
4 garlic cloves, peeled and crushed
Salt to taste
1 scotch bonnet pepper, chopped with seeds
½ x 900g packet frozen mixed vegetables
2-3 tablespoon cooking oil

METHOD

1. Heat oil in a heavy base frying pan and add in the beef pieces. Fry to seal all the sides.

2. Transfer into a casserole dish together with all the other ingredients. Season to taste with spices, add a cup of water to allow the meat to cook to required doneness.

3. Stir, cover and cook until meat and vegetables are tender. When cooked casserole should be of a semi thick consistency. Serve warm.

SUGGESTION

Other varieties of fresh vegetables can be used for this recipe. Try using other kinds of meat or chicken on the bone. You can also try using a variety of other spices. If you find scotch bonnet too hot, then use a milder alternative.

Roasted Sweet Potato Boats with Mixed Vegetables

INGREDIENTS

2-4 large sweet potatoes
2 tablespoon Greek yoghurt
Pinch of salt to taste
Pinch of chilli powder or paprika
1 teaspoon dried mixed herbs
a handful of sunflower seeds
1 green pepper, deseeded and sliced
150g grated cheddar cheese, for topping
200g frozen mixed vegetables for serving
1 teaspoon cooking oil, for extra shine on the potatoes

METHOD

1. Thoroughly scrub the sweet potatoes under running water removing all black bits. Pat to dry using a clean tea towel and lightly rub with cooking oil to add flavour, gloss and moisture.

2. Place on a baking tray and cook in a preheated oven for 30-40 minutes or until soft and well done. Check and turn sides as require.

3. Remove and set aside to cool. Use a sharp knife to carefully slice open each potato in halve lengthwise and scoop out the flesh from the centre leaving the skin intact. Put the skins aside to be filled later.

4. Place the potato flesh into a bowl and season with mixed herbs, salt, chilli powder. Add Greek yoghurt, sunflower seeds, green peppers and mix to combine. Taste and adjust seasoning as desire.

5.   Place the saved potato skins onto a baking tray and fill each skin with the seasoned potato mixture. Sprinkle with grated cheese and return into the oven to cook for 8- 10 minutes on moderate heat. Check regularly.

6.   Meanwhile boil the mix vegetables in lightly salted water to al-Dante. Drain.

7.   When the potatoes are browned, and cheese melted, remove from the oven and serve with vegetables.

SUGGESTION

Any vegetables or salad of choice can be used. Baking potato is a good alternative to sweet potato.

Grilled Chicken Fillets Mash and Lentils

INGREDIENTS

2 large chicken fillets
8-10 medium size potatoes for mash
150-200g cooked lentils, drained
1 tablespoon cooking oil, for moisture
1 teaspoon mixed dried herbs
1 teaspoon all-purpose seasoning
2 Maggi all-purpose seasoning cubes, crushed
Pinch of salt and chilli powder to taste
1 tablespoon butter to flavour the mash
½ red cabbage, shredded for serving

METHOD

1. Season the chicken fillets thoroughly with all-purpose seasoning, mixed herbs, crushed Maggi cubes, chilli powder and salt to taste. Drizzle with a small amount of oil for moisture.

2. Place under the grill for 15-20minutes on moderate heat and cook until brown on both sides and cooked through. Set aside.

3. Wash and cut potatoes into halves and boil in lightly salted water with or without the skin until tender. Drain and mash with some butter using a potato masher. Add the lentils and mix to combine.

4. Boil the cabbage in lightly salted water until tender but crunchy. Drain.

5. Slice the chicken fillets into strips and place on individual serving plates and serve with a portion of mash and cabbage.

SUGGESTION

This recipe can be adapted to own taste. You may use other alternatives available.

Mixed Fried Cabbage with Tofu

INGREDIENTS

½ red cabbage, thinly shredded
½ green cabbage, thinly shredded
1 large onion, peeled and sliced
1 small piece of ginger, peeled and grated
4garlic cloves, peeled and chopped
Salt to taste
1 x 349g packet firm tofu, cubed
1 small hot scotch bonnet pepper, crushed with or without seeds (optional)
2 Maggi all-purpose seasoning cubes, crushed
1-2 tablespoon cooking oil

METHOD

1. Put the shredded cabbage in a deep bowl and pour over boiling water. Cover to blanche for 10 minutes. Drain well and set aside.

2. Meanwhile heat the oil in a non-stick good size pot with lid. Sweat the onions, ginger and garlic over medium heat for approximately 1-2 minutes.

3. Add the cabbage. Season to taste with salt, pepper, crushed maggi cubes and all the other spices. Sprinkle with a small amount of water and stir to mix. Reduce the heat to allow it to simmer slowly without burning. Just before the cabbage is cooked add in the tofu pieces and continue to cook for a few more minutes until cabbage is tender but crunchy and tofu has absorbed all the flavours and maintained its shape. Serve warm.

SUGGESTION

Other types of cabbage can also be used in this recipe

Exciting Spinach and mushroom Rice

INGREDIENTS

500g basmati rice, uncooked
2-3 tablespoon cooking oil
1 large onion, peeled and sliced
4-6 garlic cloves, peeled and chopped
1 thumb size ginger, peeled and grated
Salt and chilli pepper to taste
2-4 all-purpose Maggi seasoning cubes. crushed
1 teaspoon curry powder
1 teaspoon dried mix herbs
1 x 200 g packet fresh spinach
175g punnet mushrooms, sliced

METHOD

1. Heat the cooking oil in a good size heavy base pot. Fry the onions, ginger and garlic for approximately 1 minute on medium heat.

2. Stir in the basmati rice and mix to coat. Pour in sufficient hot water to reach slightly above the level of the rice.

3. Season with salt, curry powder, pepper, stock cube and mix herbs to taste. Stir well to combine.

4. Cover to cook for 20-30 minutes on medium heat until the water is completely absorbed, and rice grains are tender. Just before the rice is cooked add the spinach and mushroom slices. Check if grains are done by biting into a few grains. Add water in small amounts if needed. Stir gently with a wooden spoon to mix without mashing up the grains.

5. Reduce heat at this stage to low and cover to allow any excess water in the rice to dry off and vegetables cooked. Serve warm.

SUGGESTION

You may also use other alternatives such as couscous, quinoa, millet grains.

Curried Quinoa with Kale

INGREDIENTS

400g quinoa, uncooked
1x400g red kidney beans, drained
2 handful of curly kale, chopped
1 large onions, peeled and sliced
1 thumb size ginger peeled and grated
3-5 cloves of garlic, peeled and chopped
2-4 Maggi cube all-purpose seasoning
Salt and hot chilli pepper to taste
½ teaspoon curry powder
½ teaspoon ground garam masala

METHOD

1. Cook the quinoa grains according to the instructions on the packet and then set aside.

2. Heat the oil on moderate heat without allowing it to smoke. Fry in the onions, ginger, garlic, beans and kale. Stir to combine. Reduce the heat at this stage and sprinkle with a small amount of water to prevent it from drying out and burning. Add the beans and curry spices. Season with maggi cubes, salt and chilli powder. Cover and let it simmer for approximately 2-5 minutes.

3. When the kale is soft enough add in the cooked quinoa and mix thoroughly with a wooden spoon to combine.

4. Taste and adjust seasoning as desire. Cover and continue to simmer gently on low heat stirring at intervals for a further 5-10 minutes. Serve warm.

SUGGESTION

Couscous, Rice Millet grains and Bulgar wheat can also be used as alternatives to quinoa

Unapologetic Vegetable Lasagne

INGREDIENTS

2 x 500g pack dry lasagne sheets, you can also use fresh lasagne sheets

1 large aubergine, sliced

1 x 300g punnet mushrooms, cleaned and sliced

1 large courgette, sliced

2 large green or red peppers, deseeded and sliced

2 large onions, peeled and sliced

2-3 stalks celery, washed and roughly chopped

2 x 400g chopped tomatoes

Salt and chilli pepper to taste

4-6 large garlic cloves, peeled and chopped

2-4 all-purpose Maggi seasoning cubes, crushed

1 teaspoon dried mixed herbs

2-3 tablespoon cooking oil

1 x 330 punnet cherry tomatoes for garnishing

200-300g grated mature cheddar cheeses for topping

For the White Sauce

150g table spoon all-purpose flour

80g butter or margarine

400-500ml milk

Pinch of salt and black pepper

METHOD

1. Heat the cooking oil on medium heat and fry in the onions, ginger and garlic for 1 minute. Pour in the chopped tomatoes, stir and cover to cook for 5-10 minutes until the colour starts to change to a darker red.

2. Add in all the vegetables. Season with spices to taste and cook slowly until vegetables are tender but holding their shape. Remove from heat and place on the side to cool.

3. Prepare the white sauce by heating the butter and whisking together the lour and milk over medium heat until smooth, creamy and slightly runny in consistency. If too thick add a small amount of milk or water to loosen it.

4. Lightly grease a good size oven dish and Spoon a thin layer of the white sauce over the base of the dish. Cover generously with lasagne sheets without leaving any gaps. Spoon sufficient amounts of the vegetable mixture and spread with the back of a spoon to cover evenly. Drizzle over a spoonful of the creamy white sauce. Top with a layer of lasagne and repeat the process until you have 3-4 layers of pasta depending on the number of sheets you have and the size of the dish.

5. To finish spoon the remaining white sauce over the top of the pasta to cover the entire surface. Scatter the cheese evenly over the pasta and dot the cherry tomatoes decoratively on the top. Bake in the middle of a preheated oven for 40-45 minutes until golden brown.

6. Serve warm

SUGGESTION

Any type of vegetables in season can be used as alternatives.

One-Pot Potato with chicken

INGREDIENTS

6-8 chicken pieces, washed and trimmed of all visible fat
2-3 tablespoon cooking oil
10-15 medium size potatoes, peeled and washed
1 large onions, peeled and sliced
4-6 tablespoon tomato passata
3-5 medium size carrots, washed and cut into medium size chunks
4-6 garlic cloves, peeled and chopped
1 medium size ginger, peeled and grated
2-4 Maggi all-purpose seasoning cubes, crushed
1 teaspoon curry powder
1 teaspoon dried mixed herbs
Salt and hot chilli pepper to taste

METHOD

1. Peel, wash and cut potatoes in halves and place in a deep bowl. Pour in cold water to completely submerge the potato to prevent discolouring. Leave aside.

2. Heat the oil on moderate heat in a good size pot with lid. Fry in the onions, ginger and garlic. Add the Passata and simmer gently until tomato changes to dark red in colour.

3. Pour in 2 medium cups of water. Add in the chicken pieces, potatoes, and carrots. Season to taste with the remaining spices. Stir and cover to cook for 20-30 minutes until the chicken, potatoes and carrots are tender but not falling apart and flavours well combined. It should be of a semi thick consistency when ready. Serve warm. Delicious!

SUGGESTION

Other types of vegetables can also be used for this dish

Speedy and Fragrant Couscous

INGREDIENTS

400g couscous, uncooked

2 large pieces of cooked chicken fillets, sliced

250g frozen mixed vegetable, thawed

1 large onions, peeled and sliced

2-3-star anis, finely crushed

3-5 cloves, finely crushed

½ teaspoon ground cinnamon

½ teaspoon ground coriander

2-3 Maggi all-purpose seasoning cubes, crushed

½ teaspoon chilli flakes

2-4 garlic cloves, peeled and crushed

1 small piece root ginger, peeled and chopped

2 tablespoon cooking oil

METHOD

1. Cook the couscous according to the instructions on the packet. It should be fluffy. Set aside.

2. Heat the oil in a good size pot on moderate heat and fry in all the spices. Add in the chicken fillets and vegetables. Stir to mix.

3. Add in the fluffy couscous and mix thoroughly to allow the grains to be coated in the spices. Taste and adjust seasoning as desired.

4. Cook until warmed through. Serve and enjoy.

SUGGESTION

Rice, quinoa, bulgar wheat, millet grains can also be used as alternatives.

Meat-Free Sweet Potato Pie

3-4 sweet potato, peeled and cut into halves
3-5 carrots, washed and sliced
1 leek, washed and sliced
2 celery stick, washed and sliced
2 sweet peppers, washed and sliced
2 onions, peeled and sliced
1 x 400g can chopped tomatoes
1 x 400g can red kidney beans, drained
1 small piece of ginger, chopped
3-6 garlic cloves, peeled and crushed
¼ teaspoon hot chilli powder
Salt to taste
2-3 Maggi all-purpose seasoning cubes, crushed
1 tablespoon cooking oil
200g grated cheddar cheese, for topping

METHOD

1. Boil the sweet potatoes in sufficient water until soft, drain and set aside

2. Heat the oil in a non-stick pot and fry in all the vegetables, beans and tomatoes.

3. Season to taste with all the spices. Stir to mix and cover to cook on moderate heat until sauce becomes slightly thick in consistency. You may add a small amount of water if required.

4. Mash up the sweet potatoes until smooth. Spoon the vegetable mixture into a good size pie dish and cover evenly with mash potatoes without leaving any gaps.

5. Top with cheese and cook in a moderate heated oven for 20-25 minutes until brown and warmed through. Serve warm.

SUGGESTION

Potatoes are a good alternative to sweet potatoes

Tasty Tuna Pasta Bake

INGREDIENTS

500g uncooked pasta shells
3 x 160 cans tuna in water, drained
2 x 400g can chopped tomatoes
2-3 large carrot, scrubbed and sliced
2 large onions, peeled and sliced
½ teaspoon crushed chillies
Salt to taste
2-3 Maggi all-purpose seasoning
2-3 salad tomatoes for garnishing
150-200g grated cheddar cheese for topping
1-2 tablespoon cooking oil

METHOD

1. Boil the pasta according to the instructions on the packet. Drain and set aside.

2. Heat the oil in a good size pot and fry in the onions, tuna, carrots and add the tomatoes and spices. Cook on medium heat until colour changes to darker red.

3. Add the pasta into the sauce and mix thoroughly. Transfer into an oven proof dish and top with cheese. Garnish with sliced tomatoes and place in the oven to cook on moderate heat until bubbling and starting to turn golden on top and at the edges. Serve warm and enjoy every mouthful.

8.

SUGGESTION

Bacon, sausages, salmon or any other tin fish can be used in place of tuna

PART 4

SWEET SENSATIONS

Every meal should end with something sweet.
Maybe its jelly on toast at breakfast or a small
piece of chocolate at dinner – but it always helps
my brain bring a close to the meal.

Robert Irvine

There is something about ending a meal on a sweet note that we all love and enjoy. Deserts, Afters, sweets or pudding as may be known signifies the end to any meal. Over the years I have created different types of desserts to compliment my family's mealtimes and the uniqueness of each dessert always brings a genuine feeling of excitement and satisfaction. I have also learnt over the years that dessert does not only have to be a double chocolate cake smothered in sugary sauce, but it can also be something simple, delicious and most of all made with passion. I have used some iron-boosters in the recipes, you do not have to stick with those ones. Feel free to use other varieties you prefer.

Tropical Fruits with Natural Wheat-Germ Yoghurt

INGREDIENTS

1 ripe and firm mango, peeled, stoned and cubed
¼ portion ripe paw-paw. Peeled, seeds removed and cut into chunks
¼ portion watermelon, peeled and cut into chunks
2 oranges, juiced, no seeds or 1 glass of pure orange juice
Juice from ½ a lemon
3-4 tablespoon natural or Greek yoghurt
a handful of sunflower seeds for sprinkling
Honey or golden syrup for drizzling
1 tablespoon natural wheatgerm for dusting

METHOD

1. Combine all the fruit chunks in a large bowl. Pour over the orange and lemon juice and stir gently to coat.

2. Mix the yoghurt and wheatgerm in a separate bowl. Add in the fruits and stir to combine.

3. Spoon the fruit mixture neatly into individual fruit bowls or tall glasses.

4. Sprinkle with sunflower seeds. Drizzle lightly with honey.

5. Serve at once or chill until when needed.

SUGGESTION

Any other tropical fruits can be used. Tin fruits can also be used for convenience.

Fruit Cocktail Jelly

INGREDIENTS

2 x 135g block strawberry jelly or any flavour
1 x 400g can fruit cocktail drained or any fresh fruit, sliced
500 ml of warm water
Portion of natural or Greek yoghurt for serving
A handful of mixed seeds, for sprinkling

METHOD

1. Unwrap jelly block and place in a good size deep Pyrex bowl with lid

2. Pour in the warm water and stir using a fork until completely dissolved. Add in additional water if require. Be careful not to add too much water otherwise it will not set properly.

3. Gently slide in the fruit cocktail without causing any spillage. Stir to mix and refrigerate for approximately 3-4 hours or overnight to set. When ready jelly should be of a wobbly texture and firm to touch.

4. Serve as needed with a sprinkle of mixed seeds.

SUGGESTION

Any flavour of jelly can be used. Also try using other varieties of fresh or tin fruits. Ice cream or whipped cream can also be used for serving.

Spiced Baked Apples

INGREDIENTS

2 large cooking apples
200g mixed dried fruits
Juice from ½ a lemon, no seeds
1 teaspoon ground cinnamon or nutmeg
1 tablespoon castor or granulated sugar
Portion of readymade custard or vanilla ice cream to serve

METHOD

1. Wash and carefully remove the core and any dark bits from each apple using a pointed knife without removing the skin.

2. Place on a foiled lined baking tray and sprinkle all over with lemon juice. Lightly rub with cinnamon using clean hands.

3. Stuff the centre of each apple with mixed dried fruits and sprinkle with sugar. Shove in the middle of the oven and cook on moderate heat for 30-40 minutes until soft but still holding its shape. Insert a knife or skewer in the middle to check for doneness.

4. Remove from the oven and transfer into a serving bowl. Warm up the readymade custard and pour over the apples. Serve warm.

SUGGESTION

Any other dried fruits can be used as good alternatives in this recipe.

Dark Chocolate Chip and Banana Muffins

INGREDIENTS

250gall-purpose flour
2 ripe bananas
100g castor sugar
1x 100g packet dark chocolate, roughly crushed
2 teaspoon baking powder
¼ teaspoon baking soda
Pinch of salt
3 tablespoon natural yoghurt
2 eggs
125ml vegetable oil
1 teaspoon lemon juice
1 teaspoon grated nutmeg or vanilla extract
A handful of porridge oats for sprinkling

METHOD

1. Preheat the oven on moderate heat and line a 12-hole regular muffin tray with paper cases and set aside.

2. Peel the bananas and put in a large bowl. Mash with a potato masher or a fork.

3. Add in all the wet ingredients to the banana mixture and stir to combine set aside.

4. In a separate bowl mix together all the dry ingredients and add to the wet mixture. Add in the crushed chocolate pieces. Mix until thoroughly blended scraping mixture from all sides of the bowl. Batter should be of a dropping consistency and should fall off the spatula with ease when held upright firmly. You may add an extra tablespoon of natural yoghurt or milk if required to obtain the correct consistency.

5. Use a regular ice cream scope to neatly fill each muffin case to the halfway mark. Sprinkle the top generously with porridge oats.

6. Bake in a moderately heated oven for 20-25 minutes until well risen and springy to touch. Insert a skewer in the middle of the muffin to check for doneness. A dry clean skewer will mean it is ready otherwise put it back in the oven for a few more minutes.

7. When ready remove from the oven and leave to cool on a rack. Serve or keep in a container for later.

SUGGESTION

150g of currants or dried mixed fruits can be used in place of dark chocolate. You can also bake cake in a normal cake tin, but it will take a little longer to cook

No-Bake Strawberry Cheese Cake

For the base

1 packet digestive biscuits
150g sunflower seeds
2-3 full tablespoon runny honey or golden syrup

For the filling

2 x 280gsoft cream cheese
300 ml double cream
1 teaspoon lemon juice
1 teaspoon vanilla flavour
1 tablespoon icing sugar

For the topping

1x 340g punnet strawberries, washed and sliced
3tablespoon strawberry jams
1 tablespoon cocoa powder, for dusting

METHOD

1. Crush the biscuits using a food processor until you have fine breadcrumbs. If you do not have a food processor you can use are-sealable plastic bag and a rolling pin.

2. Pour into a deep bowl. Add in the sunflower seeds and honey. stir well to bind.

3. Transfer into a lined spring-form loose bottom cake tin. Spread to cover the base of the tin using clean hands or the back of a spoon to press down into a flat and firm layer. Place in the fridge for 1-2 hours to set.

4. Prepare the filling by mixing together the cream cheese, icing sugar, vanilla and lemon until soft smooth and silky in appearance. Leave in the fridge to cool.

5. In a separate bowl whip up the double cream until soft peaks are formed. Remove the cream cheese mixture from the fridge and carefully fold in the whipped cream.

6. Remove the biscuit base from the fridge pour the filling on top and spread to cover the surface smoothly using a spatula or the back of the spoon. Make sure there are no bubbles. Refrigerate for approximately 3-4 hours to set firmly.

7. Prepare the topping by combining the sliced strawberries with strawberry jam in a bowl and stir to thoroughly coat. When the cheesecake is set remove from the fridge and top neatly with the strawberries. Dust with cocoa. Slice in portions and serve. Yummy!

SUGGESTION

Ginger nut biscuits can also be used as an alternative to digestive biscuits.

Indulging Apple Crumble

For the crumble

300gall-purpose flour
100g porridge Oats
60g soft Butter or margarine

For the filling

4-6 large Cooking apples, sliced
100g Sultanas or raisins
1-2 tablespoon of sugar, plus extra for sprinkling
1 teaspoon ground nutmeg or ground cinnamon
Pinch of salt
1 teaspoon lemon juice
Vanilla ice cream or whipped cream for serving

METHOD

1. Place the sliced apples in a bowl. Sprinkle with lemon juice. Sugar, nutmeg, and toss to coat. Add dried fruits and mix. Tip into a shallow greased oven proof dish and spread to cover the bottom. Set aside.

2. Prepare the filling by mixing the flour, porridge oats, pinch of salt and butter together into a breadcrumb-like appearance.

3. Pour sufficient crumble mixture over the apples and spread with a fork or clean hands to cover evenly. Sprinkle with extra sugar if desire.

4. Place in a moderately heated oven and cook slowly for 20-30 minutes until top is golden and crunchy and apples are tender. Check by insetting a knife or skewer through the apples.

5. When cooked leave to rest for 5 minutes to let off some steam before serving in portions with some ice cream.

SUGGESTION

Any fruits in season or of choice can be used. Tin fruits can also be used for convenience

Coconut and Dark Chocolate Chip Frozen Yoghurt

INGREDIENTS

150g desiccated coconut
1 x 150g pack dark chocolate, finely crushed
1 x 500g pot natural Greek yoghurt
2 tablespoon clear honey
1 teaspoon lemon juice
1 teaspoon vanilla flavour

METHOD

1. Drain the water from the top of the yoghurt and scoop into a deep medium size bowl. Whisk until smooth.

2. Add in the crushed chocolate pieces, desiccated coconut, honey, lemon juice and vanilla. Whisk thoroughly to combine. Consistency should be soft.

3. Transfer the mixture into individual freezer friendly containers of any shape or design cover with cling film and freeze for a few hours or overnight until hard. When ready to consume take it out from the freezer and leave for a few minutes to obtain a soft scoop. Serve as needed.

SUGGESTION

You can use any type of natural yoghurt and add other iron boosting alternatives you may desire. Blended berries, strawberry, raspberry, blueberry are good alternatives to dark chocolate.

Colourful Fruit Salad

INGREDIENTS

200g punnet strawberries, washed
200g punnet blueberries, washed
2 apples, sliced
10-12 tin prunes
2 pears, sliced
Juice from half a lemon, no seeds
1 tall glass of pure orange juice

METHOD

1. Put all the fruits into a deep clean bowl. Pour in the orange and lemon juice.

2. Stir well to combine. Spoon the fruit mixture into individual fruit bowls and serve or you may choose to chill in the fridge for when needed.

SUGGESTION

Any fruits of choice or in season can be used for this recipe.

Stewed Berries with Cream

INGREDIENTS

200g strawberries
200g raspberries'
200g blueberries
1 teaspoon fresh lemon juice
1 teaspoon sugar or clear honey
1 x 500g pot double cream, whipped
Natural wheatgerm for sprinkling

METHOD

1. Place fruits in a non-stick frying pan over low heat. Add in the lemon juice and sugar and bring to a gentle simmer stirring constantly.

2. Cook until fruits are soft and broken down. The consistency should lightly coat the spoon but not dry or burnt and should drop off the spoon when held upright.

3. Leave to the side to completely cool. Meanwhile whisk the double cream until soft peaks are formed.

4. Neatly scoop a tablespoon of stewed berries into individual tall glasses, top with sufficient cream and sprinkle with mixed seeds. Repeat the process to achieve two alternating layers of fruit and cream. Serve at once or chill and serve when required.

5. Sprinkle with any iron-booster of choice, if desire.

SUGGESTION

Frozen fruits are also good for this recipe.

Roasted Seasonal Fruits

INGREDIENTS

4 ripe and hard pears, halved and cored
4 ripe and hard apricots, halved and stoned
4 ripe and sweet apples, quartered and seeds removed
4 seedless tangerine or Satsuma peeled and segmented
Juice of half a lemon, no seeds
1 teaspoon cinnamon powder or nutmeg
1 tablespoon castor sugar or molasses
1x 500g pot natural Greek yoghurt or crème fraiche for serving
1-2 tablespoons of natural wheat germ for sprinkling

METHOD

1. Place all the fruits in a clean bowl, Sprinkle with lemon juice, cinnamon powder, sugar and mix well to coat.

2. Transfer into an oven proof dish and scatter using a wooden spoon to cover the bottom evenly.

3. Cover with foil and bake in a preheated oven on moderate heat for 20-25 minutes. Check and remove foil halfway through to allow fruits to brown.

4. When cooked fruits should be tender but not mushy. Leave to cool.

5. Spoon into individual bowls and top with a spoonful of Greek yoghurt or cream and a sprinkle of natural wheat germ. Serve.

SUGGESTION

Any selection of fruits of choice can be used. Readymade custard can also be used for serving

PART 5

THIRST QUENCHERS

There are two reasons for drinking: one is, when you are thirsty, to cure: the other is when you are not thirsty to prevent it.

Tomas Love Peacock

I enjoy having a refreshing drink whatever the weather. I find fruit and vegetable base drinks very nourishing and filling – a healthy breakfast option and a perfect start to my day. Making smoothies are a great way for me to infuse my body with nutrients from natural food source sand maintain a healthy digestive system. Join me in sharing some of my favourite iron boosting drinks recipes.

Refreshing Spinach Drink

INGREDIENTS

1 x 200g pack washed baby spinach leaves
1 full tall glass of fresh orange juice
1 tablespoon lemon juice
½ glass of cold water
1 teaspoon clear honey or golden syrup (optional)
1 teaspoon spirulina powder or natural wheatgerm
A handful of ice cubes

METHOD

1. Place the washed spinach leaves in a liquidiser, blender or smoothie maker.

2. Pour in the orange juice, lemon juice, water, honey, spirulina powder and blend until smooth. Scrap the sides to ensure all the leaves get blended. You may add a small amount of water if you desire.

3. Add in the ice and blitz for approximately 3-5 seconds to crush.

4. Pour into separate glasses and serve immediately or chill until when needed.

Carrot and Beetroot Smoothie

INGREDIENTS

3 medium size carrots
1 ball of cooked beetroot, sliced
1 teaspoon clear honey or golden syrup
1 tablespoon natural yoghurt
1-2 teaspoon lemon juice
I full glass of cold water

METHOD

1. Scrub and wash the carrots thoroughly. Cut into small pieces and put in a high powdered blender. Add in the beetroot, lemon juice, honey, yoghurt and water.

2. Blend until smooth. Add more water if require. The consistency should be how you prefer it. Add water if needed.

3. Pour into separate glasses and serve or chill for later.

Heavenly Smoothie

INGREDIENTS

1 Banana, peeled and sliced
½ ripe avocado, skin removed and stoned
a handful of kale
Juice from ½ a lemon, no seeds
1 tin pineapple chunks in juice, any size
1 teaspoon natural wheat germ or spirulina
1 teaspoon clear honey or golden syrup
1 full tall glass of cold water, to blend

METHOD

1. Put all the ingredients in a high-powered blender and blend until smooth.

2. Add water as required to get your desired consistency. Serve immediately or chill for later.

Morning Glory

INGREDIENTS

1 conference pear, sliced
2 apples, quartered with no seeds
1 celery stick
½ cucumber, sliced
5-8 pitted prunes
a handful of watercress
1 tablespoon natural yoghurt
1 teaspoon clear honey
1 tablespoon natural wheat germ or spirulina
Sufficient water to blend

METHOD

1. Put all the ingredients into a blender and blend until smooth.

2. Add water as required to obtain your desired consistency and serve or chill until when needed.

Tropical Passion

INGREDIENTS

1 tin pineapple chunks in juice
1 ripe mango, peeled stoned and sliced
¼ paw-paw, peeled and sliced
2 passion fruits, scooped out
1 tablespoon lemon juice
2 tablespoon natural yoghurt
A handful of sunflower seeds
Sufficient water to blend

METHOD

1. Put all the fruits in a blender and blend with sufficient water until smooth.

2. Pour into glasses and serve or chill until needed.

Start- My-Day Smoothie

INGREDIENTS

a handful of blueberries, washed
a handful of strawberry, washed
2 kiwis, peeled and sliced
1 banana, peeled and sliced
1 tablespoon lemon juice
1 tablespoon natural yoghurt
Sufficient water

METHOD

1. Put all the ingredients together in a high-powered blender with water.

2. Blend until smooth. Serve or chill for later.

Fruits in Season Smoothie

INGREDIENTS

2 crispy and sweet apples, sliced
2 ripe conference pears, core removed and sliced
2 ripe kiwis, peeled and sliced
1 ripe banana, sliced
1-2 tablespoon natural yoghurt
1 tablespoon natural wheat germ or spirulina powder
A drizzle of clear honey
Juice from ½ a lemon, no seeds
1 full glass of cold water
A handful of ice cubes

METHOD

1. Place all the ingredients in a blender or smoothie maker and blend until smooth in appearance and to desired consistency. Check and add more water if needed.

2. Throw in a handful of ice cubes and blitz for 3-5 seconds to crush.

3. Pour the smoothie into individual glasses and serve or chill for later.

Warm Dark Cocoa Drink

INGREDIENTS

500ml pasteurised or fresh milk
1 tablespoon dark cocoa powder
1-2 tablespoon caster sugar or clear honey
½ teaspoon grated nutmeg
A dollop of double cream for serving

METHOD

1. Put the milk in a saucepan and bring to a gentle simmer on medium heat. Stir constantly to prevent it from boiling over. Keep an eye on the heat and reduce heat as soon as it starts to boil.

2. As it simmers add the cocoa powder, sugar and nutmeg. Whisk until the cocoa powder has completely dissolved and all ingredients blended. Mixture should be hot but not boiling. Taste and adjust sugar or cocoa as desire. Whisk vigorously to get a frothy finish.

3. Pour into individual serving mugs. Top with a dollop of whipped cream and serve warm. Enjoy!

Fresh Pine apple and Watermelon Drink

INGREDIENTS

1 small fresh and ripe pineapple, peeled and sliced
¼ portion of watermelon, peeled and sliced
Juice from ½ a lemon
1tablespoon natural wheatgerm powder
1 glass of cold water

METHOD

1. Peel the skin from the pineapple using a sharp knife. Remove all black spots and stem. Slice into small chunks. Peel and cut watermelon into chunks. Place all fruits in a blender or juicer add in lemon juice, natural wheatgerm and water. Do not add too much water because the water melon and pineapple will produce a lot of their own juice.

2. Blend until smooth and serve at once or chill for later.

Adam and Eve Drink

INGREDIENTS

3 apples quartered and cored

3 passion fruits, halved and scooped out

1 teaspoon clear honey

1 tablespoon natural yoghurt

1 teaspoon spirulina or wheat germ

1 tablespoon fresh lemon juice

Sufficient water to blend

METHOD

1. Combine all the fruit and ingredients in a blender and blend until smooth. You may add ice cubes and blitz if desire.

2. Pour into individual glasses and serve or chill until when needed.

PART 6

HOW I ATE ON A TYPICAL DAY

Breakfast

Breakfast is a must for me. I never skip this part of my day. I always make time for it with no excuses. Try it and you would find that you do not need to say yes please! when the biscuit barrel is doing its rounds in the office or to pop to the shops for some sugary or fatty snacks.

1 small bowl of bran flakes with semi-skimmed milk a piece of fruit and a glass of orange juice ora warm drink. I like to have fresh lemon tea.

OR

1 small sachet of porridge oats (no sugar or honey because it has already been added to the oats) and a generous sprinkle of natural wheat germ and 1 banana or orange

OR

1 tall glass of fruit and vegetable base smoothie or any smoothie from my recipe selection

OR

A fruit bowl of seasonal fruits in natural yoghurt with wheat germ

Mid-morning

1-2 pieces of citrus fruit or 2 carrots

Any fruit or herbal tea

Light Meal

Quinoa tuna salad or any selection from my favourite light meal recipes

I small pot of fruit yoghurt

Main Meal

Portion of dry fried spicy ox liver with a portion of boiled white rice (1 cook spoon)

Plenty of steamed mixed vegetables or salad

Dessert

Portion of apple crumble with a scoop of ice cream or any other dessert from the recipe selection.

MY TIPS ON HOW I MANAGED IRON DEFICIENCY ANEAMIA FOR A BETTER WELL-BEING

There are several things we can all do to help keep ourselves healthy, happy and active. Whatever you choose to do will depend on your motivation, desire and ability to make a positive change in your life. In my case it was my desire and will-power that became the driving force in my journey to getting well. My desperation to get my life back to 'normal' was overwhelming. Here with some of my tips for a better well-being and hope it works for you as it did for me.

SELF EDUCATION AND TAKING RESPONSIBILTY OF MY HEALTH

When we are sick or unwell we always try to look for a quick cure to make us feel better again. As we all know, nobody likes being sick and when we do we all wish for a magic wand and pray for instant recovery. We tend to forget that the healing process is gradual and usually requires a lot of patience. In my case I received an excellent care from my medical team but knew I had to take some responsibility for my own health and recovery. Biblically we are reminded that "God helps those who help themselves" and with that in mind I was very determined to make some positive lifestyle changes. It became my mission to fight iron deficiency anaemia by whatever means possible. I began to read extensively about the condition to gain more understanding and that enabled me to see my condition in a positive light. I learnt about things I could do to improve my confidence, mood and motivation. I read about other people's stories, feedback from forums and got some iron boosting recipe ideas. This gave me more courage knowing I was not alone. This was truly an eye opener and the way forward for me. I am glad I did.

ADHERING TO MY MEDICATION AND FOLLOWING DOCTOR'S ADVICE

I made sure that I took my prescribed medication religiously and followed the advice of my medical team. I kept up with my follow-up and review appointments and during the consultation I would ask as many questions as I was able to. I always prepared my questions before hand by writing them down on a note pad and because of reading extensively I was never short of questions. By doing this I was able to get clarification and assurance for any doubts I had. With the knowledge gained I was able to manage my condition effectively and confidently. It is so true that knowledge is power and a great tool.

MAKING ADJUSTMENTS TO MY DIET

I adjusted my diet by cooking and eating a wide variety of natural iron-boosting foods whilst maintaining a healthy and balanced diet. I also incorporated some fibre into my diet to help with constipation because of taking iron tablets. I love food and so not shy when it comes to trying out new foods territories. I found this a great way to add variety, eliminate food monotony and boredom. I am happy I made those changes to my diet and today I still make a conscious effort to eat healthily adding moderate amounts of leafy vegetables and salad, fruits, pulses, grains and poultry – my delicious transformation is how I call it.

EXTRA BOOST FROM IRON-BOOSTERS

I added a variety of different iron boosters to all the foods that I ate from breakfast to desserts. I found interesting ways of incorporating them into my meals, snacks or drinks and my taste bud adjusted well to the different tastes after a while. We may not always like the taste of certain foods, but I believe that if you must consume them for the benefit of your health then there is very little room for choice and in my case my health took priority over all. It certainly helped with getting my haemoglobin to acceptable levels.

BALANCING MYTIME AND ENERGY

Planning and managing my time well was important to me because that way I was able to stretch my energy levels to the maximum. Planning and organising my daily activities in advance was very important. I grouped all the energy consuming activities such as cooking, housekeeping, ironing and laundry for the mornings when temperatures are cooler, and I felt fresh with energy. That way I was able to achieve a lot without feeling completely burnt out. I also made sure not to over work or over stretch myself in any one day by delegating some of the tasks to other family members instead of trying to do everything on my own. This worked magic for me as I became less tired. I have kept on using this balance of energy strategy and don't have any regrets.

POSITIVE AND BENEFICIAL LIFESTYLE CHANGES

Changing some of my long-term lifestyle routines was very hard but as an important requirement to my well-being goal I had to lock up all my excuses. I never used to have a rest or nap during the day but that became my priority because I found that it boosted my mood. The changes I had already made in my diet showed some fantastic results and I was feeling better within myself. I also enjoyed walking in the park and around my local area which I found very refreshing. Being outdoors was my 'me-time' I still do my regular brisk walking a few days a week combined with using my stationary home bike bought from a charity shop and this continues to keep me fit.

SUPPORT FROM MY FAMILY AND CLOSE FRIENDS

The support I got from my family and close friends was amazing. It kept me in high spirits with little time to think about my condition. Support is very essential because it shows that other people care about your well-being. In my case I felt loved, reassured and motivated. I believe it contributed hugely to my recovery.

TEMPORARY CHANGES TO MY WORKING HOURS

My condition interfered massively with my ability to carry out simple task at work and at home. I struggled with simple work tasks but was lucky because my work colleagues were very understanding and helpful. I was given light duties and time to rest when I needed to. I requested for a temporary reduction of my work hours which also helped in taking away some of the pressures and stress I felt. Many employers are very accommodating and would listen to your health concerns and grant your request. It is always good to talk. I am happy to say that since my full recovery work has been back to normal and my performance has been excellent. Hurrah!

GOOD NIGHT AND SWEET DREAMS

Nothing beats a good sleep and there is no doubt that getting enough sleep helps to keep our body's vitalised. I had to establish a regular sleep routine and practised some relaxation techniques which I got from the internet. I also learnt to completely switch off my mind and gadgets when in the bedroom. I bought a small radio for my bedroom which was permanently tuned on low volume on

Classic FM – my bedtime lullaby station that provided me with relaxing and calming music and always sent me off to sleep like a baby in a cot. (I still use the radio) and my husband has gotten used to having a radio in the bedroom and enjoys listening to the music as it sends him off to sleep too after a long working day. This has helped improved my sleep and believe me I am enjoying every moment and always look forward to bedtime. As you read this and think you are experiencing difficulties sleeping you can try my tip and if you are not a fan of classical music you can have it tuned on whatever music you prefer. It may be just what you need to make your trip to 'slumber city' an enjoyable one. Will be waiting for any feedbacks.

KEEPING ON THE MOVE

It was hard to find the motivation to keep physically active and, on the move, but when I concentrated on the benefits to my health I did not look back. I started with low intensity exercise by brisk walking to my local park, shops and anywhere within reasonable distance. I also worked out to a low intensity aerobic dance video twice a week. I picked up pace and as I got fitter, it became more enjoyable. You do not have to join the gym or spend lots of money to get fit because there are plenty of free open space activities that can do the job. I would advise you to choose whatever you are happy and comfortable doing. Ensure you vary your activities to maintain consistency and motivation for best results. Check out your local community and home storage for that dust-covered exercise equipment you may have forgotten about. Its free and cheaper than the gym.

MAINTAINING A FASHION SENSE

I enjoy receiving compliments about the way I look, and dress so put a lot of effort into looking good with a light touch of make up too because it makes me feel happy. Receiving compliments from others is always an added boost to my confidence. I always make a conscious effort to maintain a smart and elegant appearance without having to spend huge amounts of money by buying items on sale. I mix and match bright colours in lovely combinations and stay clear from the dark colours especially black. It can be easy to get stuck in the black colour dress zone and forget that there are other beautiful and uplifting colours. Just because you may be leaving with a condition does not automatically puts a full-stop to your fashion sense. That's how I see it. Playing around with different colours was a mood-boosting experience for me. I felt excited and stayed positive.

SETTING NEW CHALLENGES AND LEARNING NEW THINGS

Pushing myself out of my comfort zone to try new things was a real struggle. With the realisation that life is not a dress rehearsal I began trying out lots of new and exciting activities. I went to a Zumba class, learned new dance moves and made new friends. I also attended a Pilates and yoga classes for beginners but to be honest found it tricky because it involved serious twisting, bending and stretching of the body which can be difficult and painful because it requires your body to be flexible. I would not consider myself to be very flexible that's why I found it hard - flexible to an extent is how I would describe it. Maybe if I would have stuck with it for much longer I would have certainly passed the flexibility test. It may be different for you. Give it a try. Another activity which I found very relaxing was having a neck, back and shoulder massage which I booked as part of a spa package. It was an unforgettable experience and would recommend this to anyone. I continue to plan and indulge in this as my well-deserved treat. Who wouldn't? I also got recommendations from close friends and family to try out Tai Chi and aqua classes but did not find the time to try them out. Maybe you can and if you do please let us know on the feedback page. I am glad I had these fantastic experiences and felt happy because it took my mind away from my condition. I started looking forward to the weekly Zumba classes and other mood lifting activities. It was worth it. My advice to anyone will be to come out of the sofa or the house and try something you have never done before. Set new challenges. Comfort zones are barriers to our progress and killers to our motivation. Get up and act like I did.

PLANNING A GETAWAY

A relaxation weekend break outside my usual environment was an important and exciting step I took. My visit to family members in the North of England was a welcome break from my normal routine. Planning and booking ahead is a strategy that makes it affordable and achievable. A getaway break does not have to be jetting off to some exotic and expensive location. There are several affordable and exciting places within the United Kingdom accessible by coach or train and may also be the case for many other beautiful countries around the world depending on where you are living. Taking a break is refreshing for our mental well-being. If you have not tried this before I will suggest you do and you will notice the difference.

SOME KEY POINTS TO REMEMBER

1. The recipes in this book serve 2-4 persons and, in some case, more. This is because I mostly cook for more than two people coming from an extended African family and the members of my family also enjoy eating a little bit more than a moderate size portion. I have used estimates in some cases because I was taught how to cook by my mother, aunties and grandmother who never measured any ingredients. Eyeballing was how it was done and surprising it was always spot on. You can double or reduce the ingredients used according to the number of people you are cooking for. In my household there always must be extras just in case a family member comes by unannounced (Part of the African culture).

2. We are all different and may react differently to certain foods or food groups. Always check with your doctor for any allergic reaction to foods or ingredients before trying out the recipes in this book particularly the recipes which contains nuts.

3. Always check the dates on the packets of fresh foods before using. Food should be of correct texture, colour and smell. Ensure the seal on the packets of fresh vegetables, meat and fish is not broken. Also check tin foods for dates, dents and rust. If in doubt do not use it.

4. Thoroughly rinse out vegetables under running water particularly leafy vegetables and salads to get rid of sand and any unwanted guests that may possibly find their way into your dish. I have had some unpleasant surprises in the past while rinsing out vegetables.

5. Always bear in mind that cooking times and cooking heat may vary according to the different models of cooking equipment used. If in doubt, follow the instructions of the manufacturer and adjust as required.

6. The recipes in this book can be adaptable. Foods and ingredients can be swapped for available or convenient iron boosting alternatives. There is always room for flexibility. Feel free to put your own twist into it.

7. I have used iron boosters in some of the recipes because they are a concentrated source of vital nutrients needed by our bodies and can also be added to almost any food we eat or drink. In some of the recipes I have used spirulina and maca root powder these can be a bit pricey for the quantity you get. You do not have to use them. You can use other less costly alternatives such as natural wheat germ, wheat bran, oat bran sunflower seeds, dried fruits or any others you may know. Do some research and see what you come up with. If you do know some good ones that I have not mentioned in the book, please feel free to tell me when you leave a review or on Amazon my author page. We are constantly learning from each other.

8. Whatever the case may be for you either to boost your iron levels or to gain knowledge just enjoy cooking and eating what you like or fancy in moderation. Do not hold back in trying out the recipes and putting your own twist to it. HAPPY COOKING!

CONCLUSION

My journey to take control of iron deficiency anaemia (IDA) has not been without its challenges and fear of the unknown. Like most people I carried on for a long time without having adequate knowledge of how to identify the symptoms of IDA as they may be like other common illnesses. I was anaemic throughout my pregnancies and was on medication which helped. I was given the all clear and thought that was it. But as it happened, it was not to be the end as I had no idea my levels went down again unnoticed for a good few years. It's all too common to ignore messages from our bodies such as persistent tiredness or headache blaming it on work stress and other daily activities. This is the most common excuse used in the United Kingdom and probably in other parts of the world, but the truth is that it is not every day that we do work excessively hard as we claim. What about those days that we do very little but still feel tired and exhausted? These are the times I am talking about. I cannot find any reason why we do this but as a woman I am tempted to lean more towards the popular believe that women are very good at looking after everyone else except themselves and most women will agree with me on this. I have chosen to share my story, experience, tips and some of the recipes that helped me to boost my iron levels for a better well-being with the hope that it will provide ideas and information to other people who may be going through the same problem and not be aware of it.

As with any story you may be eager to know what happened afterwards and where I am now with my condition. Well! I did very well with maintaining a balanced diet with lots of iron boosting natural foods which impressed my medical practitioner who took me off my iron tablets in September 2015 a year after my diagnosis because my haemoglobin levels had gone up to an impressive and safe 14.3 Hurrah! And in March 2016 I underwent surgery to remove fibroids – My unwanted guests as I called them. I no longer suffer from constant tiredness or fatigue and have stopped craving for ice. I have carried on eating sensibly and feel revitalised. This entire experience has taught me never to ignore the messages from my body and to always listen to what my body is telling me.

My question to you is?

Are you listening to your body enough?

Do you recognise any of the symptoms on my list?

Do you suspect that you may be anaemic?

If so, please do not put it off any longer. Leave the excuses and book a consultation with your doctor as soon as possible to discuss your concerns. I am not a medical practitioner and so cannot give advice on any medical condition. I can only recommend that you seek professional help as soon as possible. My aim is to spread awareness, educate, inspire and motivate others to take responsibility of their health and make informed choices. If I can get one person who reads this book and gain some useful information from it then my job is done. The information in this book is based on my personal experience with Iron Deficiency Anaemia. I have made my experience as detailed as possible, so you don't have to worry about medical terms or generic information however if you recognise yourself in my story or know someone who is experiencing any of the symptoms I have highlighted then you need to seek medical advice immediately. On the other hand, if you already have the condition then the recipes and tips in this book may be useful knowledge for you or others you may know that have the condition. Let's spread the word, let's shine the light on Iron Deficiency Anaemia. I made the effort and it made a difference just by making changes to my diet and lifestyle. You can too!

I wish you good health

I wish you happiness

I wish you luck

For more simple, tasty, and delicious iron boosting recipes visit my food blog **kitchentalks1.blogspot.co.uk**

USEFUL INFORMATION

The following food items and ingredients used in some of the recipes can be bought from any African supermarket, Ethic food stores or Health stores:

From Ethnic food store:

Plantains, green or ripe

Powdered crayfish or shrimps

Maggi stock cubes or alternative Knorr aromat Seasoning or any other stock cubes you prefer

Maggi all-purpose seasoning sauce

From Health Stores:

Molasses pure cane sweetener

Spirulina Powder and any other iron-boosters

AKNOWLEDGEMENTS

I owe sincere gratitude to all my close family members who encouraged and supported me to write this book especially my sister in-law Mrs Gina Nganje who gave me a lot of support, recipe ideas, proof-read my manuscript and was always there at those times I felt like giving up the project. I would also like to thank my niece Malaika Nganje (Student Editor) who took her time to read through and made all the necessary corrections. I sincerely thank all my family and friends who took the time to sample the different recipes giving me constructive feedback.

A final thanks to my lovely children Lesley-Ashley Nganje and Joseph-Patrick Nganje (J.P.C Jnr) who supported me all the way particularly with the technicalities of the computer. Not forgetting my husband James Omondi Okoth who was always there for me and supported me through the challenging times. To all I say, "merci beaucoup je suis reconnaissant."

ABOUT THE AUTHOR

Cathy Nganje is a qualified Health Promotion officer (BSc Health Promotion from Middlesex University UK) a Mother, Wife, Auntie, Home Cook and Food Blogger. She works with sexual health charities on HIV prevention and other sexually transmitted infections. She also has experience working in  the social care sector and as a CELTA qualified Esol Tutor. Cathy has a deep interest in cooking and takes pride in creating delicious and vibrant recipes with spicy, flavour-packed and aromatic characters – an inspiration from her African background and culture.

Her diagnosis with Iron Deficiency Anaemia (IDA) forced her into changing her diet to eating more iron boosting foods to combat anaemia. Her iron-boosting recipes helped her in her recovery and she hope that by sharing her story it will also inspire someone else who may be struggling to find useful information on anaemia. This book will provide you with useful knowledge, tips and recipe ideas on overcoming Iron Deficiency Anaemia. Cathy strongly believes that one of the best ways to improve anaemic symptoms is by cooking and eating natural foods which generally have no side effects. Her passion for promoting good health remains her driving force.

Printed in Great Britain
by Amazon

49853066R00086